BIBLE SEEDS

*A Simple Study-Devotional for
Growing in God's Word*

BIBLE SEEDS

A Simple Study-Devotional for Growing in God's Word

STARBURST PUBLISHERS

P.O. Box 4123 Lancaster, PA 17604
www.starburstpublishers.com

Visit www.starburstpublishers.com.

CREDITS:
Edited by Deb Strubel
Cover design by Richmond & Williams
Text design and composition by Booksetters

First printing, March 2001
ISBN: 1-892016-44-3
Library of Congress Catalog Number: 00-108571
Printed in USA

Introduction

Seeds aren't meant to stay small and dormant. They are designed to soften and grow into luscious greens, vegetables, flowers, and trees. Likewise, the Word of God is not to lie on the shelf. It was given by God to take root in our hearts and to bud and blossom into godly attitudes and actions.

Just as seeds are small, so *Bible Seeds* is a small, self-contained study-devotional for beginners and mature Christians. More than a devotional and not as heavy or time consuming as some Bible studies, one lesson will take about five minutes. Don't worry if you don't know much about the Bible. The creators of the *God's Word for the Biblically-Inept*™ series had you in mind when they developed this book.

Begin each three-page lesson by reading the verse or "seed" from God's Word. Then read the main lesson text. The "Dig Deeper" word study at the bottom of the first page gives additional insight into the meaning of a significant word in the verse. (If you are the studious type, go ahead and read the word study *before* you read the main lesson.) Just don't miss these nuggets of truth.

The "Background Bulb" explains additional biblical or historical information to help you better understand the day's seed. The "Weed and Water" feature highlights how you can apply the lesson to your life. The "Sprout and Scatter" feature details ways you can nurture friends and family as you live the biblical principles.

Grab a pen or pencil and answer the "Think about it" questions. Then write your own ending for the "Prayer Pot." Finish each lesson by reading the final thought. And congratulate yourself on studying God's Word. It's fast and easy. *Bible Seeds* is a great place to start growing in God's Word.

The writers of this book are women from all circumstances—single, married, divorced, or widowed; childless; mothers of toddlers to teens; grandmothers; and stay-at-home and business women. It is our prayer that as you read these lessons, you will feel comforted and encouraged as your faith is strengthened.

—Deb Strubel

Growing Roots

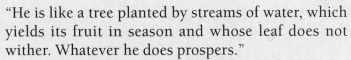

"He is like a tree planted by streams of water, which yields its fruit in season and whose leaf does not wither. Whatever he does prospers."

Psalm 1:3

Children draw the cutest pictures of trees. The trunks are usually wide and strong and covered by a circle of healthy, plentiful leaves. This is the kind of tree pictured by the psalmist, a tree planted by the water—robust, strong, and green.

If you stand under a massive tree you cannot see the roots, but they are the secret of the tree's beauty and strength. Our beauty and strength comes from the hidden part of our life too. Time alone with God forms our roots.

Roots bring life-giving water to a tree. Water is essential, or the tree will die. Jesus said, "But whoever drinks the water I give him will never thirst. Indeed, the water I give him will become in him a spring of water welling up to eternal life" (John 4:14). Our relationship with Jesus keeps us supplied with living water.

A tree grows little by little, daily inching upward. It isn't a sudden wonder like a mushroom that springs up overnight yet

Dig Deeper:

The verb "plant" actually means to transplant. To plant is to cause to take root. To transplant also means to take from one environment to another. God has transplanted us out of our self-centered way of living so that we can grow and be fruitful for him.

withers away at the first sign of the sun. A tree can withstand the heat of the sun because of its strong root system. When we have well-watered roots that are sunk deep into the reservoir of God's faithfulness, we will be like a tree that stands strong by the river.

Weed & Water:

The psalmist promises that a person who is planted firmly by the water will succeed. This promise is not a blank check to be filled in as we want, but it is a promise for spiritual prosperity, discernment, and godly character. Neither does it mean that we will never face adversity or failure. In fact, God often engineers failure and brings success—his kind of success.

Sprout & Scatter:

In the last part of this seed, the psalmist moves from the root to the fruit. When we are planted firmly in a relationship with God, he will produce fruit in our lives. Galatians 5:22–23 lists the fruit of the spirit, which we will have if our roots are strong: "But the fruit of the Spirit is love, joy, peace, patience, kindness, goodness, faithfulness, gentleness and self-control. Against such things there is no law." Having such qualities will cause us to be a blessing to our friends and family.

Think about it:

What is God's definition of success?

A person who is planted firmly by the water will succeed. God's kind of success. Amen. So be it.

How can you make your roots stronger today?

Time alone with God who strengthens me inside.

Prayer Pot:

Lord, I ask you to make my roots strong by . . .

Time with you giving your strength inside me. The roots of the spirit are strong. Having such qualities will cause to be a blessing to Christians, family, friends. Hallelujah! Thank you Jesus. Praise The Lord. Amen. So be it.

A fountain, a tree, and your tongue all have sources that cannot be seen.

Letting Go

Today's Seed

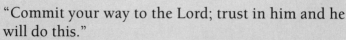

"Commit your way to the Lord; trust in him and he will do this."

Psalm 37:5

Do you ever wake in the middle of the night, overwhelmed with some unsolvable problem? Are your days consumed with wondering what you can do to fix it? Do you believe that it is your responsibility to find a solution?

If so, you are not alone. But don't give up in despair. There is a way to find relief in the midst of the most trying circumstances.

David was in such situations many times. King Saul and many of his associates were jealous of David. They conspired against him, causing him to run and hide. Sometimes he was betrayed by those he trusted. But David never gave up because he discovered the secret of letting go. He committed his problems to the Lord and gained a new perspective that he was not alone. He could trust God to care for him.

And we can do the same.

Dig Deeper:

The Greek word for "commit" is *prasso*. It means to carry into action deliberately. It is an act of our will, not our emotions.

Weed & Water:

Take that overwhelming problem, commit it to the Lord, and gain a new perspective. That is, by a deliberate act of your will, speak aloud your situation, and see yourself holding it in your hand. Lift your hand and your problem up to the Lord. Then, with open palm, turn your hand upside down and let your problem drop into God's outstretched hands. Don't wait for God to reach down and remove the problem from your upheld hand. Let it go! Commit it to the Lord, hands down . . . palms open . . . holding onto nothing.

Sprout & Scatter:

Others around us are struggling with their own problems. As we learn to commit our problems to the Lord, we will live a more peaceful life. We will be less frantic when bad things happen because we know God is taking care of us. How we live despite having problems will invite curiosity from others. This may lead to their questioning us about what is different. We can share the difference giving our burdens to the Lord makes in our lives. So we will not only live a more peaceful life, we will also be able to help others find peace through committing their problems to the Lord.

Think about it:

What problems are keeping you on the run as David was from his enemies?

Too much work, more Work in the Prep Kitchen at work, car Working every Sunday. I want all Sundays off NO A-7 P.M to 6 p.m

What action will you take to commit these problems to the Lord? *Speak about situationby. Give them to the Lord*

Prayer Pot:

Dear God, help me to let go, hands down, of . . .

all my problems, worries Work Schedule burdens, Marital problems Getting car Fixed Finding a mate to love me and sleep with me have sex intercourse as Bad likes it children, paid vacation to my spouse we go 2 weeks, finances, money problems

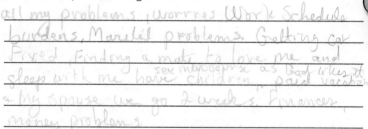

Letting go of our problems lets God overtake them.

Be Guilt Free

> "Let us draw near to God with a sincere heart in full assurance of faith, having our hearts sprinkled to cleanse us from a guilty conscience and having our bodies washed with pure water."
>
> Hebrews 10:22

The morning starts with a rush. The alarm doesn't go off. The coffeemaker overflows. The outfit we planned to wear is in the wash. The heel breaks on our shoe. The kids are fussing. The car's gas tank is near empty. All great excuses for not going to church. It's too much of an effort. We'd never make it on time anyway. So there! We're not going. Then the guilt sets in. That's not exactly drawing near to God.

Hebrews tells us that every day we'll be challenged to obey God. Sometimes Sundays are the hardest. One mother of five is positive that the devil works overtime on Sunday mornings!

We're also told that we need to "have full assurance of faith"—faith that our sins are forgiven. Because of Christ and his death on the cross, we can be sure that when we confess our

Dig Deeper:

The Greek word for "draw near" is *proserchomai*, which means to approach God, as in entering the presence of God through Jesus.

sins and our guilt, we will be cleansed through the blood of Jesus Christ.

To draw close to God we need a sincere heart, faith in God, and a guilt-free conscience. We feel guilty for many more reasons than just not going to church—guilt for what we've said or done, or what we've *not* said or done. Guilt is hard to get rid of on our own, but we don't need to feel guilt for forgiven sins. Christ paid the full price of our sin for us. Believers can have complete confidence that their sins are forgiven because they are trusting in Christ. We can be completely cleansed—guilt free.

Weed & Water:

Often when we are overwhelmed with continued guilt for something, it is because *we* cannot forgive ourselves. We believe we are above the depth of whatever sin we have done. We are shocked and can't accept that we could be so "terrible." God already knows how deeply we can sin. He has forgiven us. Chances are those around us already know how "terrible" we can be too—and they have forgiven us. All that's left is for us to forgive ourselves.

Sprout & Scatter:

Once Jesus has washed away our sins and we put our guilt behind us, the writer of Hebrews 23–25 encourages us to do four things: (1) "Let us hold unswervingly to . . . hope;" (2) "Let us consider how we may spur one another on toward love and good deeds;" (3) "Let us not give up meeting together;" and (4) "Let us encourage one another." Doing these things will benefit others.

Think about it:

When you think of entering into the presence of God, what do you think of doing or saying?

Worship, praise, love

For what do you feel guilty that God has already forgiven you?

Missing church regularly.

Prayer Pot:

Lord, help me to meet the challenges of each day, especially . . .

Not to give up meeting together.

God will cleanse our guilt, and we can hold onto that hope.

Together in Everything

Today's
Seed

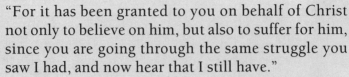

"For it has been granted to you on behalf of Christ not only to believe on him, but also to suffer for him, since you are going through the same struggle you saw I had, and now hear that I still have."

Philippians 1:29–30

There's something comforting about discovering that someone has experienced what we are going through—whether it's moving to a different state or dealing with cancer. The closer their situation is to ours the more we feel drawn to him or her. The best comfort usually comes from people whose lives have been touched by similar circumstances.

Paul reminded the Philippians that he had gone through what they were facing—persecution for being a Christian. In fact, he was sitting in prison because of his faith. They probably had heard that Paul was in prison, and they may have been worried about him. This letter would have put their fears to rest. Paul was managing well. He was not depressed—in fact, he was joyful and confident.

Paul's attitude could encourage his readers. Even if the conflict with Paul's enemies was fierce, even if he had fears, the Philippians could follow Paul's excellent example. And so can we.

Dig Deeper:
The Greek language uses one word, *agon*, for "the same struggle." Paul uses this word in other letters to describe hardships, conflicts, and much contention. The English word "agony" comes from this root.

Weed & Water:

Our salvation is a gift. According to this seed, our being chosen to suffer for Christ's sake is also a gift. Since such suffering is a gift, it implies the presence of a Giver in charge of designing and delivering the gift to the recipient. And that means God has complete charge of our circumstances. There is purpose and meaning behind our hardships.

Sprout & Scatter:

All true believers are involved in the same conflict that caused hardships for Paul and the Philippians. Through the power of the Holy Spirit we are fighting against the forces of evil. Some of us have tougher struggles and face more persecution than the rest of us. But regardless of those differences, we can be united by the same grace that saves us all.

When we are in the midst of agony, it's hard to think about others. But others are watching us. How we handle the difficulty, regardless of what it is, can be an encouragement or a stumbling block. We can comfort others with the comfort we receive from kneeling before Christ and pouring out our hearts to him. We can point others to Christ and his love.

Think about it:

How would receiving Paul's letter have comforted the Philippians?

Follow his example.

_____

_____

How do you feel when you think of persecution for Christ's sake as a gift?

Comfortable

_____

_____

Prayer Pot:

Lord, I am in agony about . . .

Persecution, working on Sunday(s) working 11:00 A.M. - 7 P.M. 10 A - 6 P. Putting more work on Prop. Ook Chart 8-4 Busy days. Holidays

_____

_____

_____

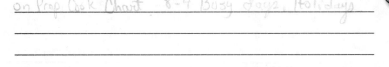

Christ allows us to be broken, so we may be bound together with others in the unity of love for God.

Surviving Betrayal

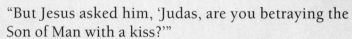

Today's Seed

> "But Jesus asked him, 'Judas, are you betraying the Son of Man with a kiss?'"
>
> Luke 22:48

Probably nothing shocks us more than betrayal. Why? Because in order for the incident to be labeled betrayal, it must involve someone close to us.

We expect strangers not to care and possibly to treat us badly. But not close friends! That's why we call them "friends." We depend on and confide in our friends, putting them in the very position to be able to betray us if things go awry. When betrayal does happen—an indiscreetly shared secret, a stolen idea, a confidential comment disclosed—our reaction often "betrays" how much unlike Christ we actually are.

Jesus was betrayed by one of his closest associates, arrested, and taken by an angry crowd to an illegal trial. The strangest part about the whole thing was how calm Jesus was. Even though the situation looked bad, Jesus knew who he was and why he had come. Jesus stayed focused on his mission—to love sinners.

Dig Deeper:

The Greek word for "betray" comes from two words—*para* meaning near, nearby, the relation of immediate vicinity or proximity and *didomi,* to give. Only someone nearby can give the hurt of betrayal.

In the same way, when we know who we are in Christ, there's no reason to collapse or seek revenge when things go wrong in our relationships. Sure, we feel angry. But we can control our behavior and stay calm. We can focus our mind on being like Christ.

God has called us to become new. He wants our reactions to become like his own. Ephesians 4:23–24 says, "Be made new in the attitude of your minds; and . . . put on the new self, created to be like God in true righteousness and holiness." Even if friends betray us, we can respond righteously because we know who we are in Christ.

Background Bulb:

Judas met Jesus in the Garden of Gethsemane. The arresting officers had told Judas that they wanted to find Jesus away from the crowds. Judas knew where Jesus hung out. The officers needed Judas to point Jesus out to them discreetly. Judas used a kiss, the sign of a close relationship, to let them know who Jesus was.

Weed & Water:

Recognizing we live in a sinful world should help us have thicker skin if we feel betrayed. Like Jesus, we can say, "Father, forgive them." OK, it's hard, but letting it go, placing our hurt in the hands of Jesus, will bring freedom and peace into our lives. Recognizing how we feel when we are betrayed should also help us steer clear of serving up this hurt to others. Finally, if we say we are Christians but our actions are the same as nonbelievers, we too are guilty of betraying Christ with a kiss.

Think about it:

What was Jesus' reaction when he was betrayed?

Calm

What was your reaction when you were betrayed?

Angry

How can you make things right with a person you have betrayed?

Respond righteously.

Prayer Pot:

Lord, help me to forgive the betrayal of . . .

Christ, my more friends, close relationships
children, family anyone, everyone, others

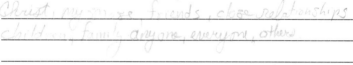

God's love is never accompanied by betrayal.

Follow the Leader

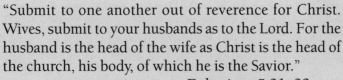

"Submit to one another out of reverence for Christ.
Wives, submit to your husbands as to the Lord. For the
husband is the head of the wife as Christ is the head of
the church, his body, of which he is the Savior."

Ephesians 5:21–23

In today's seed we are all called to "submit to one another." This
verse sets up the next portion of Scripture. Three everyday relationships are discussed in Ephesians 5:22–6:9: wives and husbands, children and parents, slaves and masters. The first party is
always commanded to submit and obey. The second party is also
to show submission by serving and concerning themselves with
the first party. In a marriage, the husband and wife are to submit
to one another.

Marriage is a picture of Christ's relationship with his church.
Just as Jesus is the head of the body, so husbands are the head, or
leader, of their wives. Some husbands may like that role and fulfill it well. Others may resent being a leader and shirk their role
at every opportunity.

Men and women have an equal relationship with God. First
Peter 3:7 says we are "fellow heirs" of God's grace. Submission

Dig Deeper:
The Greek word for "head" is *kephale,* meaning authority and direction. This is the role Christ has over the
church, and it is the role husbands have been given in
marriage.

does not make women lesser people! Husbands and wives are equal in value to the kingdom of God, but within marriage we have different functions. Men are created to lead their homes and love their wives in the same way Christ loved the church. Jesus loved the church so much that he gave his life for it. Husbands have a big responsibility. Women are their husband's helpmate and are to respect their husbands.

Submission is not being a doormat. It is not allowing behaviors contrary to God's commands to continue in your home. It is not taking on a second-class role. It is simply this: allowing and respecting your husband's position as the family leader without usurping that authority by doing things behind his back, allowing the children to disobey his wishes, or demanding your way every time.

Biblical submission is strength harnessed.

Background Bulb:

When today's seed says to submit "as to the Lord" it is not saying we submit to our husbands the same way as we do to Christ. That would be impossible, as our husbands are not perfect as Christ is. What it is saying is that our submission to our husbands is an act of service to Christ. It is our calling.

Sprout & Scatter:

There is tremendous power in biblical submission. Through acknowledging his leadership and supporting him every day, wives can empower their husbands to be confident, mature, and responsible leaders within their homes.

Think about it:

How do you feel about submitting to your husband as the leader of the family?

Stuck

List some instances when you think submission is important.

having children, pay bills,

Prayer Pot:

Father, help me to recognize my husband's leadership in . . .

our marriage, home.

Follow the leader!

God's Motherly Care

Today's Seed

"As a mother comforts her child, so will I comfort you; and you will be comforted over Jerusalem."
Isaiah 66:13

Scripture usually portrays God as a father. We expect him to be a father to the fatherless, and a husband to the widow. But we don't usually think of God as our mother. That makes this seed interesting and especially comforting.

As women, our maternal nature dictates that we take on the job of nurturing and comforting everyone else. From birth to death, women are the ones in charge of caring for all that ail.

When our motherly instincts have been stretched beyond their ability—who's to mother us? It can seem as if no one truly understands how we feel or what we are going through. We're tired, hurting, and we just want to climb into our mother's lap and have a good cry. We want our mother to say, "There, there, it will be OK."

We can be encouraged because God obviously does know how we feel. Not only is he our refuge and strength, but also he is as a mother to us. If we truly want to find comfort, all we have to do

Dig Deeper:

The word for "comfort" means to breathe deeply as a physical sign of comfort. This meaning occurs about sixty-five times in the Bible. God often shows his compassion for his people with warmth and tenderness.

is take God at his word. He understands our fears, heartache, and heartbreak. He loves us with a deep love and compassion—like a mother.

Background Bulb:
Women had greater rights in Israel than in other ancient society. A wife in Israel was viewed as more than a child bearer. She was an important partner with her husband. Among God's people, a mother's impact on her children was great. This is the position that God has given women: to have great impact on his children and to love with tenderness and strength.

Sprout & Scatter:
Many of us don't live near extended family. Instead of feeling sorry for yourself, use this as an opportunity to help other women. We can comfort and encourage each other, reaching across generations. We can be a mother to a younger woman, or a grandmother to a young girl. Ask God to pair you with another woman for companionship and mothering.

Think about it:

List some motherly comforts.

- *Comfort*
- *breathe*

In what way does God comfort you?

Warm and tenderness, strength.

How are they the same as motherly comforts? How are they different?

No This position God gives is greater

Prayer Pot:

Dear Lord, give me the caring soul of a mother . . .

Thank you in Jesus name, Amen

God cares for you like a mother.

The Gift of Children

Today's Seed

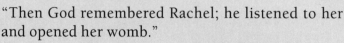

"Then God remembered Rachel; he listened to her and opened her womb."

Genesis 30:22

As you read this seed, you too may be praying that God would remember you and open your womb.

For those of us that are not able to conceive, it can take a long time and a lot of trials before we realize that just because God doesn't bless us with a child of our own does not mean he has forgotten us.

We will have to grieve not only being childless, but also that we will never be grandmothers. That is something we may not think about until our friends start having grandchildren. We need to remember what a gracious God we have. He takes away our deepest hurts and replaces them with an everlasting joy, if we allow him the opportunity.

Recognizing that childlessness may be God's plan is hard. But sometimes God has other plans for us—plans that he considers more important than our own desires. Accepting his plan with a joyful heart can be difficult.

Dig Deeper:

The Hebrew word for "remember" is *zakar,* which means to be mindful, to be aware. In the Bible "remember" is used to express concern and to act with loving care. Our Father in heaven always remembers and cares for us.

As we allow God to work in and through our lives, we will recognize that we have a choice. We can choose to let the things that happen to us make us better or bitter. Acceptance and trust in the Lord are key to making the right choice. Each experience he plans for us is designed to help us become better. It is a privilege to be a part of God's perfect plan, and a privilege to be remembered by such an awesome God.

Background Bulb:

When Sarah was well beyond the baby-bearing stage, God promised her a child. She laughed. And, yet, she could not resist "helping" God accomplish this plan. She gave her maid to her husband and had a surrogate son through their relationship. Later that lack of trust caused pain to Sarah's whole family. As we struggle through disappointing times, it can be difficult to wait on God's timing. Remember that he is mindful of you and his timing is perfect.

Sprout & Scatter:

If God grants us children of our own, we can train them. If God does not give us our own children, he often places us near children who need extra care. Special relationships are possible with nieces, nephews, godchildren, neighbors, and the kids and teens at church or our local school. We can become the trusted friend a teen turns to as she and her mom struggle through the growing-up years. Or we can be a big sister to an inner-city child. These relationships would not be possible if we had children of our own. It is an honor to be a part of their lives.

Think about it:

What are you waiting on God to remember?

_____

_____

_____

_____

Who could you mentor while you wait?

Special relationships

_____

_____

_____

Prayer Pot:

Father, help me to pray . . . Thy kingdom come, thy will be done . . .

Amen

_____

_____

_____

_____

_____

Even in the darkest moments, God remembers to give gifts to his children.

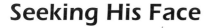

Seeking His Face

Today's Seed

"I lift up my eyes to you, to you whose throne is in heaven."

Psalm 123:1

Have you ever searched for an important face in the crowd? Perhaps this happened when you walked into a darkened movie theater or when you were lost in a mob at the stadium. You may catch a glimpse of the person, only to have them disappear again.

Is God's face equally hard for you to locate? Or is he standing out above the crowd, looking directly at you when your eyes meet his? And once your eyes lock on his, are you able to maintain a steady gaze to see into his heart and soul for your life?

The psalmist who wrote today's seed was looking for God. His hope was tied to his knowledge that if he looked hard enough, he would witness God's mercy in his lifetime. God never hides his face from us. He does not play peekaboo, discounting our present condition.

When we have difficulty seeing God, it is often because we have focused our eyes on someone or something else. Our point of focus shifts too easily. Material possessions, self-worth, and

Dig Deeper:

The Hebrew word for "lift up," *nasa,* has many meanings and uses. We can raise up our head, face, eyes, or voice to the Lord. That means we get our focus off ourselves.

personal fulfillment—all considered "noble" causes in today's society—have clouded our eyes. Unfortunately, we fixate on God for shorter periods of time and are quickly distracted by these so-called causes.

God's Word repeatedly reminds us to seek his face. The greatest blessing of seeking God's face may be that he also has his eyes trained on each one of us.

Background Bulb:

Psalm 34:15 says, "The eye of the Lord is upon them that fear him, upon them that hope in his mercy." How he does this we may never know, but we can trust in the Almighty's ability to watch over us. His majestic throne is in heaven, not here on earth.

Weed & Water:

How can we seek the face of the Lord? God reveals himself through his written Word, through prayer, and through fellowship with himself and other believers. Eventually we won't have to look so hard to find his face. And we'll find that he was there all along. So keep seeking!

Think about it:

Think about the last time you couldn't see God's face. Why couldn't you?

Distracted.

_____

_____

What benefits or blessings will come to you as a result of lifting up your eyes and seeking God's face?

Get the focus off myself.

_____

_____

Prayer Pot:

Dear Lord, I confess that my eyes . . .

on something, or someone else, I ask your

forgiveness in Jesus name Amen.

_____

_____

_____

_____

Look up, not in.

Jars of Clay

> "But we have this treasure in jars of clay to show that this all-surpassing power is from God and not from us."
>
> 2 Corinthians 4:7

Jars of clay—dull, plain, and drab. Yet Paul used the term to describe us. Doesn't sound too complimentary, does it?

We are nothing more than a clay jar—not too beautiful. When we consider how useful a jar is, however, we get a good picture of what Paul meant. A clay jar is a container to hold items. We are designed to hold treasures. In fact, our Christianity should cause people to be baffled about how an ordinary woman with nothing outstanding about her can have such remarkable traits. Our lives should make others wonder.

When we weather a storm, stay calm in difficulty, or get along with troublesome people, others are amazed. They marvel when we are happy and radiant in the middle of pressures and trials. Thanksgiving, praise, joy, strength, faith, and love are the treasures that overflow from our clay pot. They are the miracles of the Christian life, which spill over into the lives of the people around us.

Dig Deeper:

The Greek word for "clay" is *ostrakinos,* which means earthenware or made from clay with the added suggestion of frailty. Though we are weak, God allows us to hold his treasures.

We need to refocus our thinking on the treasures inside the jar, not the jar itself. Rejoice in what we have, not what we lack. Our lives are full of treasures: God's light, God's power, true values, promises from God, and confidence in him. When we realize what we hold, we no longer worry over how we look.

Background Bulb:

The Bible often uses clay to describe human beings. We were formed from the dust of the ground which Job called clay in Job 33:6. Isaiah said, "Yet, O Lord, you are our Father. We are the clay, you are the potter; we are all the work of your hand" (Isaiah 64:8). God formed us and continues to mold us daily. He is developing us so that we will be able to hold the treasures that he wants the world to have.

Sprout & Scatter:

The most important treasure that we hold in our clay jar is the gospel of Jesus Christ. When people notice the good things about our lives such as joy, peace, patience, and kindness, it is our opportunity to tell them the good news about Jesus and his offer of salvation. Nothing we could offer is as valuable as this life-changing message. Ask yourself, "Do people know more about Jesus simply because they know me?"

Think about it:

What trait do you have that will make people wonder about your Christianity?

My life
_____
_____
_____

How can you share your treasures of joy and peace with someone today?

Worship God, Bible Study & Prayer,
_____
_____
_____

Prayer Pot:

Lord, thank you for placing the treasure of the gospel in my clay jar. Please help me to share it today with . . .

Bible Study & Pray, Buddy
_____
_____
_____
_____

The value of our life depends not on how we look but on the use we make of it.

Spin with Joy

Today's Seed

> "This is the day the Lord has made; let us rejoice and be glad in it."
>
> Psalm 118:24

What a glorious day! What? It's raining? The forecast is for the rain to turn to sleet? Then to freezing rain? With a possible two feet of snow by morning? So, what's the problem? What a glorious day! God made this day. Let's embrace it and be joyful.

There *are* days, however, when we just don't feel like rejoicing. Our lives are out of sync, and we just want to crawl into our cave and hibernate. But that's the perfect day to reread today's seed, and know that God is always here for us.

Psalm 118 is a hymn of thanksgiving, rejoicing over all God has done. It begins and ends with a call to praise, repeating this verse—"Give thanks to the Lord, for he is good; his love endures forever" (Psalm 118:1, 29). Repetition is always a clue that the repeated phrase is important.

The psalmist used this chapter to praise God for his many blessings. He thanked God for past blessings, for God's help with past struggles, for God's might, for God's love, for everlasting life,

Dig Deeper:

The Hebrew word for "rejoice" is *guwl*, which means to spin around under the influence of an emotion such as exceeding gladness, to be joyful. Allow your joyfulness to show!

for his salvation, and for God's light that shines on us all. The Psalms show us a great way to approach life.

With a little effort we can always find something for which to be thankful. And thankfulness has a way of developing into joyful celebration. We'll be enveloped in God's love, and then we'll rejoice in that love like the psalmists. Sun, rain, sleet, or snow, we can rejoice.

Weed & Water:

Each day is a gift from God. It's like a beautifully wrapped present, tied with a bow, just waiting for us to open it and see what's inside. Children opening presents on Christmas morning spin around in glee. It's so easy as adults to become self-conscious and to stop ourselves from expressing enthusiasm and joy. When no one is looking, try spinning around as you praise the Lord. You'll probably end up laughing—and that's the whole idea.

Sprout & Scatter:

Perpetually pleasant people can be annoyingly fake. But the psalmist wasn't fake. He acknowledged his troubles, and then chose to focus on God's blessings. Next time things aren't going well or the weather isn't what you had hoped for, acknowledge your difficulties. Then try humming or singing this seed. Your joyful spirit can bring joy to others.

Think about it:

How can you show that you are rejoicing in the day God has created?

Spin around and praising the Lord.

What can you do on those days when you just don't feel like rejoicing?

Ing this is the day that the Lord hath made we will rejoice and be glad in it

Prayer Pot:

Lord, I praise and thank you for . . .

Each day a gift being open to see what is inside and praising the Lord. Hallelujah! Praise th Lord Amen

Spin around with joy!

Look for a Miracle

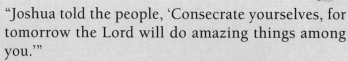

"Joshua told the people, 'Consecrate yourselves, for tomorrow the Lord will do amazing things among you.'"

Joshua 3:5

God's great love is shown in the things he does for us. He provides everything that we need every day. But most of us haven't experienced all the blessings that God has in store for us. God wants to do amazing things for us just as he did for the Israelites long ago.

Joshua gave the people of Israel a wake-up call. He warned them to get consecrated because they were about to face a major crisis when they came to the Jordan River. Since there were no boats or bridges, it would be a test of their faith like nothing before. They had heard their parents' stories about the crossing of the Red Sea. Now they would need a miracle for themselves.

When the day arrived for Israel's miracle, the priests carried the Ark into the waters of the river first. As soon as their feet touched the water, the river dried up. The people followed on dry ground. The Ark represented God. It contained the actual stone tablets of

Dig Deeper:

The Hebrew word for "consecrate" can be explained by using the words "get serious." To consecrate yourself, let go of all things frivolous and extraneous so that God can go to work.

the Ten Commandments and other symbols of God's presence such as Aaron's rod and a jar of manna. When the people followed the Ark, they were following God.

When God goes before us, amazing things happen.

Background Bulb:

After the Israelites crossed the Jordan River, they went to Jericho where they met a woman named Rahab. She told them that the news of the river drying up had reached the whole city. Now everyone was in awe of Israel because Israel's God had done this miracle. When we allow God to do amazing things in our lives, it affects everyone around us. Not only do we see the miracle, but they do too.

Weed & Water:

To see miracles, we must set the stage inwardly and outwardly by preparation, dedication, and separation. Bible studies and prayer prepare us inwardly. Anticipation of miracles is built on the knowledge of God's Word and a personal relationship with him through prayer. Once the inward preparation is underway, our outward dedication will become evident. When we've spent time with Jesus, it shows. Separation from everything that keeps us from knowing God is the final element needed. Then we are ready to see miracles. And God will not disappoint us. He will do amazing things, wonders beyond our imagination.

Think about it:

What might have happened if the Israelites hadn't consecrated themselves before this test of faith?

Might of faced a major crisis

What have you done to set the stage for God to do amazing things in your life?

Bible Study, Prayer, through prayer.

Prayer Pot:

Lord, open my eyes so that I may see the miracle of . . .

Your hand is upon us, Miracles you want
for my spouse, and me.

Miracles come after a crisis.

Faith

Today's Seed

> "Now faith is being sure of what we hope for and certain of what we do not see."
>
> Hebrews 11:1

If you've ever been in charge of an event at church, your children's school, a volunteer group, or at work, you've had to rely on others to help get things done. (Unless you're the do-it-yourself type who can't delegate! But that's another Bible seed.)

To pull off an event successfully we need to let go and share the work. We try to trust that people are doing what they've said they will do, but most likely we check to make sure. We don't have "faith" that things are being done unless we have a loyal friend who has helped before. If we have such a tested friend, then we can be certain.

The "heroes" in the Old Testament were filled with faith. When Abraham was called to go to the Promised Land, he obeyed. He had faith. He packed his belongings and started hiking, even though he didn't know where God was leading him. Amazingly, Sarah, his wife, followed. She had great faith in her husband, and she had faith in her husband's God.

Dig Deeper:

The Greek word for "faith" is *pistis,* which means the conviction of the truthfulness of God, and especially in reliance on Christ for salvation. We need to have the faith of Abraham.

Faith is a living thing, an active way of life based on the certainty that the object of our hope is trustworthy. Abraham must have proven himself to be reliable, so reliable that Sarah moved with him away from their relatives. God must have shown himself reliable to Abraham, so reliable that Abraham knew the Lord's voice and was willing to obey when God said, "Leave your country . . . I will make you into a great nation" (Genesis 12:1–2).

Background Bulb:

The first chapter of Hebrews gathers together the stories of many of the Old Testament heroes of faith from Abel and Enoch to David and Samuel. Not all the heroes, however, were triumphant over the events in their lives, but God blessed them all. God remained faithful even when they were faithless.

Weed & Water:

It's easy to talk about having faith. It's not as easy to carry through. Our faith may falter occasionally. Stuff happens, and we can get caught up in a spiral that shakes us, making us wonder—for an instant—if there truly is a God. By examining stories of God's faithfulness to past generations and by thinking about how God has given us small joys in the past, we can be assured God is in his heaven and all is right with his world . . . our world will catch up.

Think about it:

How would you define faith?

Living, great.

If your faith varies from day to day, why does it?

Things happens

Prayer Pot:

Lord, help me to let go and have faith that you . . .

all is right with his Word

Faith for the future is founded on the
faltering steps of obedience today.

Grace

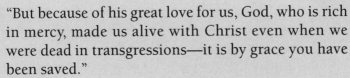

Today's Seed

> "But because of his great love for us, God, who is rich in mercy, made us alive with Christ even when we were dead in transgressions—it is by grace you have been saved."
>
> Ephesians 2:4–5

What is the difference between love, mercy, and grace? Paul describes all three in these two verses by saying that God who is rich in mercy loved us so much that he gave us grace. All three of these represent a part of God's character that caused him to provide a plan for our salvation.

When God looked down at us and saw our needy condition, he had compassion on us. Our suffering and inability to rescue ourselves from our circumstances caused him to have mercy on us. When his pity for us was coupled with his great love, he developed a plan for our freedom. Mercy is the aspect of God's love that caused him to help the miserable. Mercy and love mixed together motivated God, but they did not satisfy his holy nature.

He is a holy God, and he cannot look at sin. That's when his grace took action. Through grace, God exercised the plan to

Dig Deeper:

The Greek word *charis*, translated "grace," is the word for God's favor. His favor is different than ours. His favor is *always* accompanied by action. Our favor usually means good intentions. When God is favorable to us, we receive a blessing.

provide Jesus Christ as a substitute for our sin. Grace is the aspect of his love and mercy that moves him to forgive the guilty. Mercy and love are the why of salvation; grace is the how.

Background Bulb:

If you look for the words "grace," "mercy," and "love" in a thesaurus, it will give each word as a synonym for the other. It isn't surprising that we don't understand the difference in the words. Only those who are indwelled by the Holy Spirit can comprehend that a God of love looked down in mercy and provided grace. We can remember it this way: Mercy is God not giving us what we deserve (eternal punishment for our sins), and grace is God giving us what we don't deserve (eternal life in heaven).

Sprout & Scatter:

Receiving grace from God is a precious gift. It is the gift that keeps on giving. We don't deserve it, yet he showers grace on us. Since we have received so much grace, we can give it to others. When a friend is late, give her grace. When she hurts your feelings, give her grace. "Bear with each other and forgive whatever grievances you may have against one another. Forgive as the Lord forgave you" (Colossians 3:13–14).

Think about it:

What caused God to reach out to you in grace?

Our needy condition.

How can you share his grace with others?

Give to each other.

Prayer Pot:

Lord, thank you for your grace in . . .

forgiveing one another.

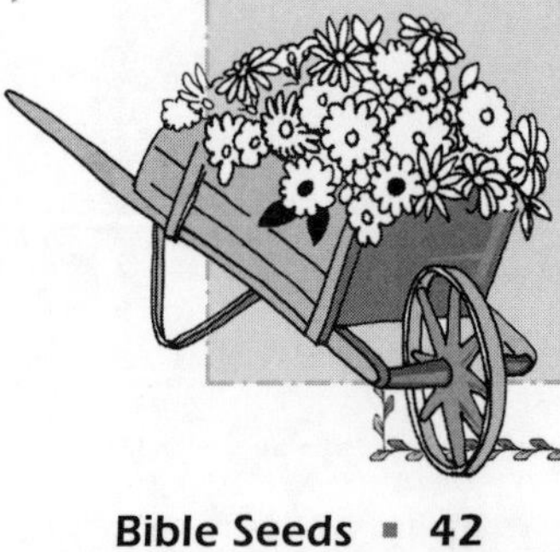

God never runs out of grace.

Everything We Need

Today's Seed

> "His divine power has given us everything we need for life and godliness through our knowledge of him who called us by his own glory and goodness."
>
> 2 Peter 1:3

Hidden in the middle of this seed is a powerful little phrase that can be easily overlooked as we hurry through our daily Bible reading. Three little words, "everything we need."

It doesn't say that God gives us some of what we need or part of what we need. It is a firm commitment; we are given "everything we need." God has given us "everything we need" through Jesus Christ. It tells us that we have been given all that we need to live life, and to live it in a godly manner.

Stop and think—what do you need right this moment? According to this promise, whatever that may be is available to you. Now there are some qualifiers to the promise. What we need comes to us from God's "divine power." Therefore, we must have received Jesus Christ as our Savior, and with that the presence of the Holy Spirit, who dwells within us, giving us power. That is the first qualifier. The second is getting to know Jesus Christ, who he

Dig Deeper:

The Greek word for "knowledge" is *ginosko*. It means to take in knowledge, to come to know, recognize, and understand. In the New Testament *ginosko* often indicates a relationship between the person knowing and the person being known.

is, how he lived, and the example and instructions he left for us. So our needs must also be in accordance with the teachings of Scripture.

Weed & Water:

Because everything we need will come through our relationship with Jesus Christ, we need to know him. The only way we can really get to know a person is to spend time with him or her. We also need to converse with him or her. So spending time with Jesus will include our reading the Bible to learn about his attributes, commands, and promises. It will also include our talking with him about our needs. In listening to him we may find him clarifying the difference between what we see as our "needs" and what he sees as our wishes, wants, and desires. Have you ever stopped to consider that God might view your "needs" differently than you view them?

Sprout & Scatter:

Many people get discouraged when they feel that God does not keep his promises. At such times they have confused their needs and God's view of their needs. As you begin to get to know God in a relationship you will understand the difference between needs and wishes or wants. Then you may be able to bring encouragement and hope to others. Matthew 6:33 reminds us: "But seek first his kingdom and his righteousness, and all these things will be given to you as well."

Think about it:

How can you get to know God better?

Received Jesus Christ as Savior how he lived, instructions he left for me. Spend time with him.

What is one "need" you have that God might see as a wish or want? _God's leading right direction, Marriage_

Physical Intimacy, Best Mate, Best Husband God's Best for me, God's plans shown What God wants for me, Singing. Talking in tongues

Prayer Pot:

Dear God, show me the difference between my needs and wants and help me to . . .

Listen to him, talking to him, view my needs Converse to him, What action to take, God's not let me being leading in the right direction in love Marriage.

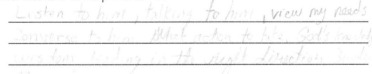

God knows our needs. He will supply.

Bubble with Zest

Today's Seed

"Never be lacking in zeal, but keep your spiritual fervor, serving the Lord."

Romans 12:11

Do you have a zest for life? Do you rise and shine in the morning with a smile on your face? What about your zest for serving the Lord?

When Paul wrote to the people of the church at Rome, he told them they had to put their religion into practice . . . not just bring it out when worshiping. We should be continually serving the Lord, bubbling over with love and spiritual zest.

Fervor is on Paul's long list for anyone who wants to shine with the joy of being a Christian. It is a list that requires us to possess sincere love, have a love of life, rejoice in hope, endure affliction, always be in prayer, provide for the needs of fellow believers, seek hospitality, bless persecutors, live peaceably with all, overcome evil with good, and more.

Seems overwhelming just thinking about it, and there goes the zest. This seed implies that we are the ones who keep our fervor up. We are apt to blame others for our problems and our lack of zeal to

Dig Deeper:

The Greek word for "fervent" is *zeo*, which means to be hot, boiling, bubbling over. Our zest for serving God should bubble over into all parts of our lives.

do what's right. Paul understood that after an initial burst of energy, it takes diligent effort to maintain a glow in serving God.

What enables us to keep our spirits up is to focus our efforts not on cheers from those around us but on the prize at the end of life. Believers have the firm hope of seeing Jesus in heaven and being united with him. Such hope enables us to persevere despite less than perfect circumstances. It's not easy. Nothing worthwhile ever is. Paul was right. We should act like serving the Lord is the most important thing in life, because it is.

Weed & Water:

Some people just naturally have more energy than others. But overcommitment can rob us of the energy we have and keep us from doing our best. Sin can also form a crust over our zest for the Lord—keeping our fervor from bubbling out. Take mental inventory of your abilities and note the things you enjoy doing. How can you focus on those things and use them to serve the Lord?

Sprout & Scatter:

Did you know that we use more muscles when we frown than when we smile? Sunday school children are taught: If you see someone without a smile, give them one of yours. We can start our day by smiling at everyone we meet—not a Cheshire cat grin, but a pleasant, friendly smile. It will be one small way of bubbling with fervor and of making a difference in the lives of those we meet.

Think about it:

What is your zest level?

Hot, boiling, bubble over.

Look back at Paul's list for believers. Which qualities do you have now, and which qualities should you work on?

Fervor, All.

Prayer Pot:

Dear Lord, help me realize I have much to get excited about in my life, such as . . .

to maintain a glow in serving God. I should act like serving the Lord. A pleasant, friendly smile each day. Thank you Jesus.

"Nothing great was ever achieved without enthusiasm."
—Ralph Waldo Emerson

Alone or Lonely?

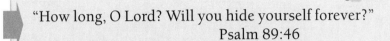

"How long, O Lord? Will you hide yourself forever?"
Psalm 89:46

There's a big difference in being alone and being lonely. When you're alone, it's just you. No one else is around. You are set apart from everything and everybody and can celebrate the quiet—joyfully.

There are times, however, when being alone makes us feel lonely. We can even be in a crowd and still feel isolated and abandoned. We may feel as the psalmist felt that God has left us or hidden himself from us.

The psalmist questioned why the Lord had seemingly abandoned his people. He was tired of waiting, and he reminded God in the next verse that he'd been searching for him but had only a short time here on earth—so hurry up! "Remember how fleeting is my life," he said. "For what futility you have created all men!" (Psalm 89:47).

When we experience lonely times, it's not that God is hiding from us but that we can't see him through our crowded life. We

Dig Deeper:

The Hebrew word for "Lord" used here is *YHWH*, or Yahweh. This name was so sacred to the Jews that they never pronounced it. Instead, they said *Adonai*, a common word for lord. When we feel lonely and question God's ways, it is good to remember to be respectful to his name.

are not alone. Loneliness can be used by God to turn our focus to him, helping us to hear what God wants. If we open our eyes and hearts to God, we can learn from lonely times and welcome times to be alone.

Background Bulb:

Psalm 89 is different from many of the psalms. Most begin with complaints and prayer and end with joy and praise. This one is the opposite. It begins by praising God's love and faithfulness and ends with questions and discouragement. *The Message* paraphrases verse 49 this way: "So where is the love you're so famous for, Lord?" David, the author of this psalm, was really feeling down.

Weed & Water:

When we feel lonely and discouraged and think that God is far away, we can learn from David's example in this psalm and talk to God. Go to God with your questions. Be honest about your feelings. While doing so, remember to respect God as Lord of the universe. Ask God to turn lonely times into loving times with him. With his help, alone time can be embraced as time to spend with God. Perhaps that's why he has allowed you to be lonely in the first place. We can actually learn to look forward to time alone.

Think about it:

Are you alone or lonely?

yes

When have you felt that God is hiding from you?

in a crowd

What will you do to turn lonely times into alone times with God?

Focus on God. Open my eyes and my heart
to hear what God wants

Prayer Pot:

Dear Lord, I feel . . .

Alone, lonely. Open my eyes, heart to what
to hear God wants. Thank you O Lord

Regardless of how you feel, God will never leave you nor forsake you.

Seeking What's Lost

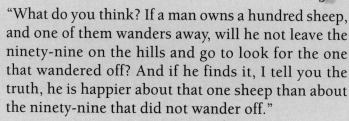

"What do you think? If a man owns a hundred sheep, and one of them wanders away, will he not leave the ninety-nine on the hills and go to look for the one that wandered off? And if he finds it, I tell you the truth, he is happier about that one sheep than about the ninety-nine that did not wander off."

Matthew 18:12–13

The garden stuff flew off the shelves. Seed packets from last year, two trowels, a hand cultivator, ball of twine and a bright green kneeling pad. . . . Where are the garden gloves? Ah ha! Here's one, but where's its mate?

The search is on. One glove is not enough, especially when spreading mulch. Five minutes later, still only one glove. Oh, well. There's a new pair in the potting shed cupboard. We'll just forget about the lost glove.

It's a good thing God's not like us. He doesn't just toss us away when we're lost. When we stray from him, he's ready and willing to come looking for us, just like the shepherd in the verses above.

Dig Deeper:

The Greek word for "wander" is *planao*, which means to roam, to go from safety, truth, or virtue. We can wander from more than physical safety when we stray from God.

Here's this shepherd. He's got ninety-nine sheep safely in the fold, but is he satisfied? Nope. He has to have all of them. He misses the one that isn't there. If we admit it, there are days when we'd be ecstatic to find ninety-nine out of the one hundred things we looked for! Amazed, even.

But not this shepherd. He loved the sheep he worked with day after day. He was concerned about that one lost lamb. He had to find it. And he searched for it until he rescued it and brought it back to the fold.

Background Bulb:

When Jesus spoke of the lost sheep, he used a familiar theme, also used in the Old Testament, that shows clearly the love of God for everyone—nonbelievers and believers alike. This parable of the lost sheep is also found in Luke 15:4–7. There it is told to the unbeliever. Here in Matthew it's told to believers. It's the same story, retold to reveal Jesus' truth to different listeners. Jesus often used parables, or stories with similes or metaphors for comparison meanings, to teach.

Weed & Water:

Sometimes things aren't lost; we just don't remember where we left them. They're here, somewhere, we tell ourselves. We may feel lost in our spiritual life. We don't know where we are, but God knows just where to look for us. God will not give up on us. Just like the shepherd, God will pursue us until he rescues us and brings us back to safety, truth, and virtue. His "flock" is not complete until we are safe in his family.

Think about it:

How have you wandered from safety, truth, or virtue?

Yes

What will you do differently now that you know you are precious to God?

Not to stray from God

Prayer Pot:

Lord, be my shepherd and keep me from straying from you because of . . . _God pursues me, rescue me_

bring me back to safety, truth and virtue.
Bring me back safe into your family. I
am precious to God. Amen. Hallelujah,
Praise the Lord.

You are precious to God.

There's No Place Like Home

Today's Seed

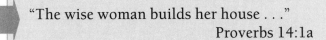

"The wise woman builds her house . . ."

Proverbs 14:1a

All women are homemakers whether they work outside the house or not. The question is, what kind of a home do we make? Is it a place to catch a few winks, eat hasty meals, and change clothing between activities? Or is it a haven, a resting place of safety, security, and love?

The home was meant to be a powerful hub for ministry. And the woman of the home was meant to be a useful servant of God—first to her family and then to the world. The home environment we create can be a source of refreshment that reenergizes us to face the world.

Our children learn the most from home. They are our most far-reaching ministry as their lives will affect the world around them for years to come. They need our time and energy to become all that God has planned for them.

Our home is also a ministry of hospitality. As we serve others, they will catch a glimpse of the humility of Christ. They will see the radiance of God on our faces and the faith-inspired love for

Dig Deeper:

The word "build" here refers not to physically constructing a house, but rather caring for and planning a household so it may flourish. A wise woman doesn't neglect her household.

each other in our actions. As people leave a home of love they cannot help but be touched and inspired.

We are all homemakers. It is not a matter of what we do as homemakers; it is a matter of catching the vision of our home as a dynamic place of ministry—first to our families and then to the world.

Weed & Water:

Creating a smooth-running home takes patience and hard work. In placing your home and family at a high priority you may need to unclutter your schedule. Slow down for a minute, and visualize the kind of home you wish to have. Jot down steps you need to take to begin creating that vision.

Sprout & Scatter:

Help children to be organized by providing simple easy-to-reach shelves and cubbies to store toys and clothes. Establish regular times when they must put things away. Sing a special cleanup song, such as, "This is the way we pick up toys" to the tune of "This is the way we wash our clothes." Create a family activity corner for keeping schedules, car keys, notes to each other, and emergency information.

Think about it:

To whom does your home minister?

Spouse, family, friends, others

What are some ways you could use your home as a ministry tool this month?

Serve others.

Prayer Pot:

Lord, let my home be a ministry by . . .

as a dynamic place first to my family.

A homemaker is a multitalented professional!

Don't Waste Time

> "Remember your Creator in the days of your youth, before the days of trouble come and the years approach when you will say, 'I find no pleasure in them.'"
>
> Ecclesiastes 12:1

Homework. Cheerleading. Term papers. Camping trips. Dishes to wash. Football and basketball games. Laundry. Movie dates. Dusting and vacuuming. Slumber parties. As students, there is so much to fill our days. There's plenty of time to get serious about God later.

Work projects. Mommy and Me Club meetings. Housework. Doctor appointments. Carpools. PTA meetings. Bake sales. Diapers to change. Spills to wipe. Exercise classes. As young mothers, there is so much to fill our days. There's plenty of time to get serious about God later.

Paying tuition. Menopause. Dealing with teenagers. Husband's midlife crisis. Saving for retirement. Training replacement at work. Remodeling the house. As midlife women, there is so much to fill our days. There's plenty of time to get serious about God later.

Dig Deeper:

The days of trouble are those in which we face natural or moral evil, adversity, affliction, calamities, displeasure, and distress. The longer we live, the more days of trouble we'll experience.

Helping to care for grandchildren. Volunteering at the library. Attending friend's children's weddings. Having grown children move back in. Learning to live on a fixed income. Health concerns. As active seniors, there is so much to fill our days. God will just have to understand why I haven't gotten real serious about church stuff.

When will you have the time?

Weed and Water:

We may *think* we can put God off till tomorrow, but there will come a time when it will be too late. We'll wish we had made time for God. And there lies the secret. We must *make* time for God by carving out or setting aside a few minutes here and there. Praise God while you shower. Tape request reminders to the mirror and pray while you fix your hair or put on makeup. Keep a Bible, devotional, or this book at work and start your day in God's Word. Write key verses on index cards and place them in a recipe holder to read while you are in the kitchen.

Sprout & Scatter:

Be careful about buying the lie that you can do everything yourself. Yes, there are lots of things that must be done. Here are two suggestions regarding your busy schedule. First, get help. It's not a weakness to ask for help, and asking before things get out of control is best. Second, say no. Give others the opportunity to get a blessing or to be a blessing by letting them perform the task you were asked to complete.

Think about it:

In what area are you lacking obedience to God?
(Examples: prayer time, personal Bible study, visiting a neighbor, etc.)

My home, work, Church. Mid-life.

What excuses have you used for neglecting God?
How can you overcome these excuses?

Work, Laundry putting others before him.
God is in control. At work fill Request
slips and turn them in before two weeks.

Prayer Pot:

Lord, thanks for creating me. Help me get serious about you
in the area of . . . _church stuff and have the time,_
regarding busy work schedule, Ask for help.
Second. When to say no. Thank you Jesus.

"Never before have we had so little
time in which to do so much."
—Franklin Delano Roosevelt,
Fireside Chat, February 23,
1942

Living Carefree

Today's Seed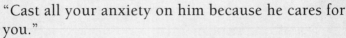

> "Cast all your anxiety on him because he cares for you."
>
> 1 Peter 5:7

Life is getting easier. At least, that's what the advertisements promise. New detergents, gadgets, and machines pledge to do all our work. But newfangled tools have a way of bringing with them new sets of problems. Casting all our problems on God is different. We can be assured of real help—not more problems—because he cares for us.

Imagine that! God, who has the whole world to manage, cares for us. What's important to us is important to him. Nothing is too big or small. What we thought we couldn't handle, he can. He takes our anxiety about friends, health, property, and jobs—even those everyday, never-ending housework chores. We live carefree because he cares for us. Everything he promises he delivers.

He will either get rid of what we fear, support us as we face it, or exchange it for his load. The good news is that his burden is light. "For my yoke is easy and my burden is light" (Matthew 11:30). What does he give us that is so light? He gives us mercy,

Dig Deeper:

The Greek word *epi* is translated "upon." It means to superimpose. You've seen those doctored photos with mix and match faces and bodies. Now picture you and your anxiety with Jesus superimposed underneath it— you and your care totally upheld by Jesus.

grace, strength, and assurance. He has already given us the tools to do everything he wants us to do. When we call to him, he gladly answers. His customer support line is never busy.

Background Bulb:

Psalm 55:22 can help us understand the concept of casting our care upon the Lord: "Cast your cares on the Lord and he will sustain you; he will never let the righteous fall." God gave us our position in life, our abilities, and our talents. He knew exactly what we needed and what we could handle. Nothing that comes our way will be too much for us because he sustains us. He has never let the righteous fall.

Weed & Water:

One of the definitions of the word "anxiety" is distraction. Life is full of distraction. It seems we can't finish a simple task like making dinner without being interrupted by something or someone. Living without care means that we don't let the distractions triumph over us and keep us from accomplishing our goals. Make a list of the distractions in your daily routine. Present the list to God asking him to keep each one from interrupting your day.

Think about it:

Look back through this lesson and list some promises of God.

- *God cares for me   1 Peter 5:7*
- *Matthew 11:30   His yoke is easy and his burden is light*
- *Psalm 55:22   God will sustain me*

How has God shown you that he really cares for you?

He gave me tools that I need.

Speaks, talks to me.

God answers me

God takes the distractions from interrupting me.

Prayer Pot:

Lord, thanks for caring about . . .

I ask God to keep each distraction

from interrupting each day.

Watching over us is not God's duty; it is his delight.

Love Versus Hate

Today's Seed

"But I tell you: Love your enemies and pray for those who persecute you."

Matthew 5:44

At the end of the day do you feel as if you've been in a battle? Surrounded by the enemy? At war with the world?

You probably have been. Our enemies are all around. From the driver who pulled out in front of you on the way home, then shook his fist at you as if *you* were the one at fault, to your boss who expects 200 percent from you and yet is stingy with praise. It's enough to make you want to throw your morning bagel at your boss—cream cheese and all!

But what good would it do? None. It might even get you fired.

When enemies are all around, remember Jesus' teaching: "Love your enemies." Bless them. Be thankful for them. Say, "I'm thankful for my boss" because it means I have a job. Say, "I'm thankful for that terrible driver" because . . . well, just because.

Dig Deeper:
The Greek word for "enemy" is *chalepos*. It means difficult, painful, grievous, and irksome. It means people who are hard to deal with, cruel, harsh, stern, and even dangerous.

Background Bulb:

Matthew chapters 5, 6, and 7 are a sermon called The Sermon on the Mount. It is the longest and fullest continued teaching from Jesus. When Jesus spoke on the mountain at Galilee, he commanded, "But I tell you love your enemies." Take note. The word is "commanded." Not suggested. Not theorized. Jesus commanded us to love our enemies. It is our duty as Christians to love our enemies—no matter how mean they are to us and to others. We need to have compassion on them and speak well of them.

Weed & Water:

In Matthew 10:28, Jesus says, "Do not be afraid of those who kill the body but cannot kill the soul. Rather, be afraid of the One who can destroy both soul and body in hell." We might not be afraid of an enemy we can handle, but loving them is impossible. There's no way to do it without God's help and power.

First, we have to want to love. Be honest with God about your feelings. Start today. Start small. Loving our enemies doesn't come naturally, although with God's help we can learn to live with them. Even if we don't see any good in them, God calls on us to love them anyway. Praying for our enemies can be one way to develop love for them.

Think about it:

Why is it easier to turn against those who persecute us rather than to love them?

I tate

How can you show your love for the difficult people you have to deal with?

Love them, Praying for them. Develope love

Prayer Pot:

God, grant me your view of my enemies. I don't feel like loving them, but . . .

with God's help learn to love with them,
Praying for them can be love to develope for them.
God sees good in them and so can I.

God causes the sun to rise on you and on your enemies. If God sees good in them, so can you.

What Now?

"If any of you lacks wisdom, he should ask God, who gives generously to all without finding fault, and it will be given to him."

James 1:5

"What will I do?" We often ask that question when confronted with a tough decision. We don't know which way to turn. We are confused and sometimes frightened. Who can we trust to give us direction in the tough issues of life?

James instructs us that the first place to turn is to God. Why do we tend to seek the answers elsewhere first? Do we think that God is not interested in all the little details of our lives? God does care. He cares about every detail. Our daily decisions are important to him. He is always ready and waiting to give guidance and direction when we ask him for wisdom.

Perhaps we don't ask God for direction because what we really want is not in line with the principles of Scripture. Perhaps we don't ask because we are afraid he might ask something from us that we are not willing to give. Or maybe, when we ask, we don't

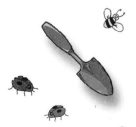

Dig Deeper:

For James, wisdom is a practical thing. It is not philosophic speculation and intellectual knowledge; it is concerned with the business of living. Christian wisdom is knowledge of the deep things of God as they apply to daily life. It is essentially practical.

really listen to hear his answer. God only wants what is best for us. He knows the future and can be trusted to direct us in the way that will ultimately bring us the greatest blessing.

Weed & Water:

When you are wrestling with decisions, turn to God for direction. Go first to your Bible. Ask yourself, "What are the principles in God's Word that apply to my situation?" Ask God, in prayer, to direct you to those passages. If you cannot find direct answers in Scripture, then turn to other Christians whose wisdom and counsel you respect. Often books written by respected Christians can give wise counsel. God works in many ways to answer our requests.

Sprout & Scatter:

As we learn to wait and trust the Lord for wisdom in living, we will become an example to others. People may seek us out for help in discerning the answers to their problems. As we grow in faith, trusting the Lord for answers to the daily problems of life, we also grow in wisdom. We can help others discover wisdom by our example of trusting God for answers.

Think about it:

Where do you need wisdom right now?

Future daily decisions, Christian Wisdom

How can you discover what God wants you to do?

Ask God in prayer to direct me to those
passages situation. Allow the Living Word
to work in many ways to answer our requests.

Prayer Pot:
Dear God, please give me wisdom for . . . _Listening As I learn and_
trust the Lord for wisdom, I will be an example
to others. As I grow in faith, trusting the Lord
for answers to the daily problems of life, I grow
in wisdom. I am an example of trusting God
for answers.

Wisdom has two parts: listening and
learning.

The Glory of God

Today's
Seed

"Then the man brought me by way of the north gate to the front of the temple. I looked and saw the glory of the Lord filling the temple of the Lord, and I fell facedown."

Ezekiel 44:4

What an awesome sight—the temple shining with the glory of God! This seed is part of Ezekiel's vision about the future. It describes the return of God's glory to the temple. The Lord is standing next to Ezekiel as he looks back at the temple. The glory of God is so intense that the temple is aglow with it even though the Lord is now standing outside.

Ezekiel saw the marvelous glory of God coming from the east gate and completely filling the temple. God's glory actually caused the entire land to radiate. In addition, it sounded like rushing water!

God is so wonderful that whatever he touches glows. God is so strong that his power makes noise. And God is so holy that when humans come face-to-face with him we have only one response:

Dig Deeper:

Shekinah is Hebrew for "that which dwells." It is a term used to indicate the special or visible presence of God. God expressed his presence in a cloudy, fiery pillar when he led the Israelites out of slavery in Egypt. These visible manifestations have been called God's "shekinah presence" or "shekinah glory."

to fall facedown like Ezekiel did and worship him. Our human eyes are not able to look at God's full glory because we are sinful. The brilliant light known as God's glory is a symbol of his awesome holiness.

Ezekiel wasn't the only Bible character to see God's shekinah glory. In Exodus we read that the Lord allowed his goodness to pass in front of Moses. When Moses came down from the mountain, his face was radiant (Exodus 34:19–20, 29). God is so holy that all who see his glory and goodness shine. Talk about leaving an impression! What kind of impression do you leave on those you encounter?

Background Bulb:

Not since the destruction of Jerusalem during the third Babylonian invasion in 586 B.C. had God's glory been present among his people. Ezekiel's vision made it clear that God's glory would return after Israel was cleansed and after the new temple had been constructed following the discipline of the end times.

Sprout & Scatter:

As representatives of God, we should clothe ourselves in goodness, compassion, kindness, humility, gentleness and patience. And although only God is holy in essence, we have the Holy Spirit dwelling in us to enable us to be an expression of his character. By living a life that reflects the essential nature of God, the believer both glorifies the Lord and serves as a beacon to others. When God's holiness and glory shines through us, those we meet are attracted to the light and drawn to Christ.

Think about it:

What are some possible results of seeing God's glory?

God touches.

Faces are radient

What things might be keeping you from shining with God's glory?

Being a beacon for others to come
to know Christ.

Prayer Pot:

Lord, your glory is too bright for me to see completely. Help me to . . .

be an expression of his character. By living
a life that reflects the essential nature of
Israel, glorify the Lord and serves as a
beacon to others. God's holiness and glory
shines through me and those are meet are attracted to
the light and drawn to Christ.

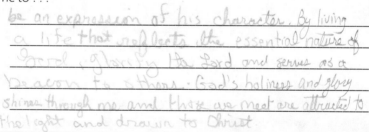

God's glory is so awesome it overpowers the darkness.

Beware!

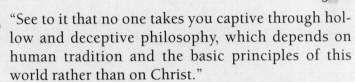

"See to it that no one takes you captive through hollow and deceptive philosophy, which depends on human tradition and the basic principles of this world rather than on Christ."

Colossians 2:8

People today actively seek spirituality. Unfortunately, they don't always look to the Bible for guidance. Books like *Conversations with God* and *The Seat of the Soul* top the national best-seller lists. These books counsel readers to find their god within. They are full of Eastern religious or New Age ideas, not biblical truth. Psychic readers on television, telephone, or the internet offer to predict the future for a price. Cults like Scientology attract high-profile entertainers who deliver their message worldwide. Seeker-sensitive churches also grow as people search for something to fill their inner void.

Sometimes the message of Christianity gets watered down. We are tempted to take a good idea here or there and add it to ideas from the Bible. Paul knew how dangerous it was to become distracted from the basic message of Jesus Christ and to get carried

Dig Deeper:

Beware! Watch Out! This is the warning Paul intended with the opening words of today's seed. Danger is ahead, and we are to take notice, pay attention, and be on the lookout.

away by the popular teachings of the time—teachings that sounded nice or made people feel good. Paul warned the Colossians to be on guard against watering down the truth of Christ or being caught in the deceptions of hollow philosophies.

Paul described how Christians should live. They are to incorporate their actions and attitudes with their faith, taking an active role in keeping their faith founded on biblical truth.

Background Bulb:

In Paul's time the church was being influenced by philosophies that were threatening the basic message that Jesus Christ is the only way to salvation. Some popular religious leaders of the day said tradition was more important than faith. Actions proved your salvation. Others said superior knowledge was the path to salvation. Still others taught that Christ was not really a human being and that sin was an illusion.

Weed & Water:

Complacency is often the culprit that causes us to be led astray. We rely on others to teach us the truth. Often we don't check what we hear with what the Bible teaches. It takes hard work to evaluate everything we hear in the light of Scripture.

Society has so emphasized being tolerant of other's beliefs that the lines between truth and falsehood have blurred. Harassment and ridicule come if we are not "politically correct." We don't want to offend others, but we fail to remember that we may offend Christ. This week search the Bible to find the truth about what you hear, do, and say. Then speak up for Christ.

Think about it:

How do your current reading and listening choices line up with the principles of God's Word?

Founded on bibical truth

_____

_____

What changes do you need to make to ensure that Jesus' teachings underlie your philosophy?

Speak up for Christ. Search the Bible.

_____

_____

Prayer Pot:

Dear God, show me what I need to . . .

find the truth about what you hear, do, and say. Then speak up for Christ.

_____

_____

_____

_____

Be aware, for complacency is a downward path.

Beating Laziness

Today's Seed

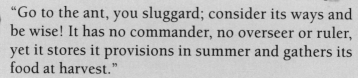

"Go to the ant, you sluggard; consider its ways and be wise! It has no commander, no overseer or ruler, yet it stores it provisions in summer and gathers its food at harvest."

Proverbs 6:6–8

If you are a typical woman, with a long to-do list, it's likely that physical laziness is not a problem for you. In fact, most of us rarely slow down. Still it is wise to consider our lives and be sure.

The writer of Proverbs suggests that we observe the ant's activities to evaluate ours. The ant has no commander yet he works. He takes initiative. Do we? The ant plans for winter by storing food for the difficult times. He plans ahead. Do we? The ant works in summer. He has his priorities right. Do we?

The ant is weak yet weakness never stops him. He works continuously to get the job done. You can see thousands of ants in a mound and not one will be idle.

If physical laziness is not our problem, then we must consider if we have another kind of laziness—a laziness of attitude. This kind of laziness ignores problems because ignoring is easier.

Dig Deeper:

The word "consider" is translated from the Hebrew word *ra'ah*, which means to behold and approve. It is the same word that is used in Genesis 1:4, which says that God saw that what he had created was good. Observing the ant helps us see a good way to live.

Attitude laziness fails to instruct children about the right way to live because it's too much bother to confront them. Attitude laziness makes excuses for not witnessing or sharing what God has done in our lives with others. It makes us give in and rationalize when we know better.

Weed & Water:

An ant has at least three traits that we need to keep from developing a lazy attitude. First, an ant is patient. It may take a long time to move a morsel of food to the mound. Second, he is persistent. When his way is blocked, he never gives up. Third, the ant has courage to come above ground to face whatever dangers are present. Developing these traits into our lives will cause us to be wise like the ant.

Sprout & Scatter:

Our attitude laziness can affect the people around us without us ever saying a word because they observe us. They will know we have a lazy attitude when they see bitterness, negativism, dishonesty, or whining. But they can learn patience, persistence, faith, and courage instead if we exhibit these traits in our activities. Just as we observe the ants, we are being observed.

Think about it:

What attitude is causing you to be lazy?

Laziness

List some ant-like traits that you need.

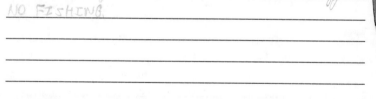

- _Faith_
- _Patience_
- _Persistent_
- _Courage_

Prayer Pot:

Lord, convict me of any areas of laziness . . .

attitude, forgive me for the times when I was lazy—
NO FISHING.

Most of us are lazier in mind than in body.

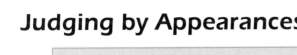

Judging by Appearances

Today's
Seed

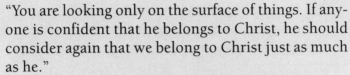

"You are looking only on the surface of things. If anyone is confident that he belongs to Christ, he should
consider again that we belong to Christ just as much
as he."

2 Corinthians 10:7

Look at that guy over there. And that young woman with him—
what color *is* her hair anyway? And those earrings and their shoes
and. . . . No matter what our age, there are people in the world
who look strange—to us.

Judging by appearances can become an everyday habit if we
allow it. With our mental critique we often condemn others. Who
are *we* to set ourselves up as judges? We forget that, perhaps,
they're judging us—and finding us lacking also.

When the apostle Paul was trying to prove himself to the
Corinthians, he accused them of looking only on the surface of
things, of judging by appearances. Paul asked, and we should
ask, too, is it right to judge people by what we see? Or think we
see? Based on appearances it's difficult to tell what a person is

Dig Deeper:
The Greek word for "judging" is *aisthesis*, meaning per-
ception and discernment, to see or understand differences. We need to look beyond the surface and forget
about judging others.

really like. Many people hide their true emotions—some under a facade of humor, others behind a prickly pear mask.

Only God knows our inner being. We can tell what a person looks like, but God can tell who a person is. First Samuel 16:7 reminds us, "The Lord does not look at the things man looks at. Man looks at the outward appearance, but the Lord looks at the heart." What does God see when he looks at you?

Background Bulb:

In the first six verses of chapter 10, Paul defends his ministry. He has been accused of not being "spiritual" enough and not having the credentials to be a true apostle. Paul doesn't mind being asked about his credentials, but he doesn't agree with the Corinthians' measuring tool. Surface things, such as a person's stage presence, speaking skills, confident claims, and authoritative manner impressed them. Paul wanted to be judged by how his ministry had affected those who had heard him, not by how he looked or spoke. He didn't want the Corinthians to be led away from truth by the next great speaker who taught unbiblical ideas.

Weed & Water:

Make an effort to open your heart and mind to people who are different from you. Look beyond the clothes, hair, language, skin color, and way they do things to find common ground. You might be surprised to find that your differences can be fascinating. You might even discover that you *like* "different."

Think about it:

On what basis did Paul want to be evaluated by the Corinthians?

outward appearances. Forget about judging them

How can you accept others who belong to Christ?

Not to be led away by the truth

Prayer Pot:

Lord, help me to look beyond the surface and see . . .

common ground.

God loves you. God loves everyone, period!

Waiting Expectantly

Today's Seed

"In the morning, O Lord, you hear my voice; in the morning I lay my requests before you and wait in expectation."

Psalm 5:3–4

Hospital waiting rooms are no fun. Some people just sit and stare at the trees beyond the glass windows. Some bury their minds in a romance novel. Others nervously pace the floor, jingling the keys in their pockets. Still others bring along their briefcases, trying to make the most of the circumstances. Occasionally, in a corner one person will comfort a companion, hugging and wiping away tears.

Waiting. We don't like it. Even if we don't have to spend time in a hospital, we are faced with waiting every day. From the ever-present lines in the grocery store and bank to waiting on God to answer our prayers, we must wait. Waiting is inevitable. But we can choose how to wait.

We can daydream like the window watcher in the hospital waiting room. Or we can immerse ourselves in unimportant things like cheap novels or TV. Some of us wait by worrying, pacing the floor of our lives while we fret over our circumstances.

Dig Deeper:

The Hebrew word for "wait" is *tsaphah*, which implies leaning forward and looking up. Waiting on God is anticipation not apathy.

God asks us to wait in hopeful expectation, believing that he will always work things out for our best. God is the Lord of the universe; yet, amazingly, he cares about every detail of our lives. Since our hope is in him, our attitude about waiting must reflect the expectancy and optimism of that hope. It is a matter of confidence in God. If you rely on him, your waiting room behavior will show it.

Weed & Water:

Getting to work while we wait on God, like the person with the briefcase, demonstrates that we believe in God's timing and wisdom. Instead of wringing your hands, busy your hands. Volunteer at your church. Take food to a shut-in. Visit someone in need. Even cleaning closets is good. Hearty activity produces healthy waiting.

Sprout & Scatter:

People all around us are hurting and in need. When we observe them waiting on God, our reaction can help or hurt. As companions comfort each other in the waiting room, we can comfort those around us who are waiting. Have mercy. Be compassionate. Give a smile and a hug. Your touch may bring God's love to a worried, waiting soul today.

Think about it:

What prayer are you waiting for God to answer?

That God will work out things for my best.

What can you do to demonstrate your hope in God?

Getting to work believe in God's timing and wisdom. Smile, give a hug.

Prayer Pot:

Lord, today I expectantly wait for you to . . .

work out things for myself, marriage, family.

Do all you can, and then wait
expectantly on God.

A Real Bargain

"He said to me: 'It is done. I am the Alpha and the Omega, the Beginning and the End. To him who is thirsty I will give to drink without cost from the spring of the water of life.'"

Revelation 21:6

We all love a sale. Two for One! Now that's a bargain! Unfortunately, sometimes we treat our prayer life as if it too were for sale. We bargain with God: "Lord, I promise I will blah, blah, blah, if you will only answer my need now!"

We are so foolish. Do we really think that we can drive a better bargain than we have already been offered? The greatest bargain of all time is not only a two-for-one deal, but it's free! It doesn't get any better than that.

Not only are we given the Creator of the universe, but also everlasting life. The Alpha and the Omega, the first and last word in all things, the creator of the universe, the Almighty God, the One in control of the world is also our loving Father. He offers us the privilege of freely drinking from the water of life—living waters that will bring everlasting life.

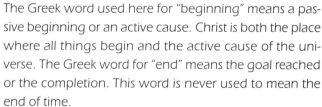

Dig Deeper:

The Greek word used here for "beginning" means a passive beginning or an active cause. Christ is both the place where all things begin and the active cause of the universe. The Greek word for "end" means the goal reached or the completion. This word is never used to mean the end of time.

Background Bulb:

Alpha and Omega are the first and last letters of the Greek alphabet. They symbolize Jesus Christ, Creator and Culminator. God the Father and Christ the Son are revealed to be both the source and the sum of all. It is interesting that this announcement is reserved until the judgment of the world is over in Revelation 21 when Christ can finally say, "It is done."

Weed & Water:

God reveals his essential nature and character by his names Alpha and Omega. We can be assured of three things: (1) God created us for his glory and purpose; (2) God sustains us in the present; and (3) God will complete what he has begun and bring us to the final goal.

When we pray, we can trust him to understand our past, be concerned about our present, and be in control of our future. It is not necessary for us to "bargain" with him to get his attention. He is present with us, committed now and forever, not only to be God but to be *our* God. When we pray, we are not to offer bargains but to offer our prayers in the name of Jesus as instructed in John 14:6: "No one comes to the Father except through me." God promises that when what we ask is within his will, we can be sure that our requests will be granted.

Think about it:

What three things can you learn from knowing that God is Alpha and Omega?

- *God created me for his purpose and glory*
- *God sustains me in the present*
- *God will complete what he began in me to the final day*

If you have bargained with God, what will you do about that?

To offer prayers in the name of Jesus.
To ask within his will

Prayer Pot:

Lord, help me remember to bring all things to you by prayer and petition, especially . . .

in the name of Jesus as he instructed
Thank you Jesus

God's greatest bargain is free and two for one; he's the Alpha and Omega.

Grandparents Are Great

Today's Seed

> "I have been reminded of your sincere faith, which first lived in your grandmother Lois and in your mother Eunice and, I am persuaded, now lives in you also."
>
> 2 Timothy 1:5

Grandparents delight in their grandchildren. In them they see the continuation of the family, and they see the future. Whether we have one or a dozen grandchildren to love, we enjoy being with them, watching them, joining in their play, and teaching them. Lots of fun surrounds grandbabies and even "grandteenagers."

Grandparents have a great opportunity to mentor the next generation. They can teach many skills and character qualities. Grandparents can read to grandchildren, helping them to love reading. Some may teach children to play baseball or soccer; others may teach them to knit or play the piano. All grandparents need to do their part in leading the young generation to Christ.

Timothy was one of the first "second-generation Christians." He learned about Christ at home through his grandmother Lois and mother Eunice—not from the disciples or Jesus himself. His grandmother and mother began their teaching of Timothy at an

Dig Deeper:

The Greek word for "sincere" is *anupokritos,* which originally meant inexperienced in the art of acting. Lois and Eunice weren't acting. Since their faith was real and not fake, Timothy learned true Christianity from them.

early age. Paul said of him, "From infancy you have known the holy Scriptures, which are able to make you wise for salvation through faith in Christ Jesus" (2 Timothy 3:15).

Although Timothy's father was not a Christian, the influence of Lois and Eunice overcame that. Timothy absorbed what he was taught and became a godly man and served the Lord well—thanks to his grandmother and mother.

Background Bulb:

Paul was alone in a Roman prison when he wrote the second letter to Timothy. He was allowed only a few visitors, but could have his writing implements. Paul encouraged Timothy to carry on the work of leading the church. This letter, more personal sounding than Paul's first letter to Timothy, became the last words of Paul. He emphasized what he felt was important: sound doctrine, faith, endurance, and love.

Sprout & Scatter:

Storybooks centered on Bible characters can be a good way to get the message of the Bible across to grandchildren. We don't have to limit our influence to our own grandchildren, though. Bible storybooks can be given to the children of friends and neighbors and to our local libraries. If your grandchildren don't live near you, volunteer to read to or listen to children at your local elementary school.

Think about it:

How do you think Lois and Eunice shared their faith with Timothy?

Real faith teaching at home at an early age.

How involved do you think grandparents should be in their grandchildren's lives? Why?

Every chance or opportunity, Real faith to share God's Word from infancy

Prayer Pot:

Dear Lord, give me the words and knowledge to share with . . .

when it is time for me and my husband to share God's Word with our children, teenager(s) grandchildren and Christian storybooks centered on Bible characterics Thank You In Jesus name, Amen.

Share God's Word with children.

Seeking Perfection

> "Because by one sacrifice he has made perfect forever those who are being made holy."
>
> Hebrews 10:14

Perfect forever! Who wouldn't want to be called perfect? Many of us have grown up believing the lie that to be truly loved by God we need to be perfect. We know intellectually that God loves us just as we are, but emotionally we often feel as if he might love us even more "if only."

"If only" we didn't lose our temper occasionally or we had more patience. Maybe you can't even identify the "if only's" in your life. They are just there in the background—vaguely making you wonder if God really can love you.

This seed holds the key to being set free from the "if only's" that keep us from experiencing God's perfect love. There are two parts to understanding this freedom. First, realize that when God looks at us, he sees us through the image of his Son. Jesus Christ's sacrifice on the cross paid the price for all our "if only's." In God's sight we are already perfect. Second, Jesus Christ has been given the task of making us holy. This is a lifetime, ongoing process.

Dig Deeper:

The Greek word for "perfect" is *teleioo*. It means to bring to an end by accomplishing or completing. This is what Christ's work on the cross did for us in the sight of God.

You and I are a work in progress. We don't have to doubt our perfection in God's sight, nor his perfect love for us. Our responsibility is to join Jesus by cooperating with him as he makes us holy.

Weed & Water:

We can't make ourselves holy or perfect. The harder we try, the more we see that it is impossible and we feel like a failure. Jesus Christ has been given the job of refining us, making us into his image. We join in the process by confessing our sins, learning from our failures, and starting again. Along the way we can have the assurance of Philippians 1:6. *The Living Bible* says it this way: "And I am sure that God who began the good work within you will keep right on helping you grow in his grace until his task within you is finally finished on that day when Jesus Christ returns."

Sprout & Scatter:

As we become free from trying to reach perfection in our own strength, we can also help others discover their freedom and perfection in Christ. Often we project our expectations of ourselves onto our friends and family. Sometimes we allow other's sins or failures to shake our faith in their salvation. When we view others, as God does, through Jesus Christ we can see that they, too, are a work in progress. Then our focus moves from condemnation to helping them discover the promise that Jesus is working to "make us holy."

Think about it:

What "if only's" keep you from believing that in God's sight you are perfect?

Do not believe "if only's".

How can understanding that you are a work in progress help you grow in his grace?

By joining Jesus cooperating with Jesus

Prayer Pot:

Dear God, help me cooperate with you in . . .

_Jesus and cooperating as Jesus makes
me holy. Thank you for that promise_

You are a work in progress.

Bend for a Promise

> "I have set my rainbow in the clouds, and it will be the sign of the covenant between me and the earth."
> Genesis 9:13

Low-hanging clouds shuffle for position in the late afternoon sky. The wind stirs the leaves, turning their silvery undersides out. The sky blackens. *Ping. Ping. Pa ping.* A few drops of rain fall. Then more and more, until it's a downpour. The rain blows across the street in sheets. Just when we think it will never stop, the sky lightens, the rain slows, and off in the distance we see the faint colors of a rainbow arching across the sky. As we watch, the colors deepen and expand. "Look," we exclaim, "a rainbow!" Perhaps we shiver with awe.

When God made the decision to flood the earth to rid it of extensive sin, he also made a way for some of his creation to be saved. Years before the flood, God directed Noah to build the ark, giving him specific plans for doing so.

When the ark was built, God opened the floodgates and wiped out everyone and everything, except for Noah, his family, and the animals he carried on the ark. After the flood, God promised

Dig Deeper:

The Hebrew word for "rainbow" is *qesheth*, which comes from the original sense of bending, as in a bow and arrow, thus a rain bow. It's a visual display of God bending his mercy around earth.

Noah that he would never again destroy the whole earth with a flood. He set a rainbow in the sky as a symbol of his promise. Each time we see a rainbow we are reminded of that promise, and we catch a glimpse of heaven.

In heaven, Revelation 4:3 says, "A rainbow, resembling an emerald, encircled [God's] throne." The rainbow around the throne of heaven means that God's promises are eternal. The green color could stand for God's mercy. God never goes back on his word.

Weed & Water:

Too often we become blasé about marvelous things. When we see a rainbow, do we shrug, saying it's just the refraction and reflection of the rays of the sun on the raindrops? Or do we remember that the rainbow was put in the sky thousands of years ago as a symbol of God's promise and as a peek into the future?

Sprout & Scatter:

Because we are human, we can forget our promises. Before making a promise, ask yourself if you are prepared to take on the responsibility of the promise. Sometimes we need visible reminders of the promises we've made to others and to God. A wedding ring is a reminder of wedding vows. Photos around our home or office are reminders of our love for family and friends. Notes on the refrigerator or on our car dash remind us of promises we've made to do something. To faithfully keep promises we have to bend our will—just like a rainbow bends around the earth—and sometimes give up our convenience.

Think about it:

How do you think Noah and his family reacted when they saw the first rainbow?

God's promise, God's mercy.

How does the idea of bending make you feel about a promise you have made?

Faithful and obedient. Loving.

Prayer Pot:

Lord, your rainbow promise makes me feel . . .

Faithful and obedient Loving, mercy, humble, meek.

In a rainbow, God bends his mercy and love around the earth.

Stuck in Stubbornness

Today's Seed

> "The Israelites are stubborn, like a stubborn heifer. How then can the Lord pasture them like lambs in a meadow?"
>
> Hosea 4:16

Stubbornness can be clearly identified in the life of a toddler. He or she resists the leading and prompting of the person watching over them. If we could peer into the heart and mind of such a child, we would probably detect an attitude that says, "I want what I want, and I want it now!" Unfortunately, we don't automatically outgrow that stubborn attitude.

The prophet Hosea had the job of reminding the Israelites to be faithful to God. He gave the people multiple warnings against idol worship and defiling themselves through pagan practices. Yet they disregarded his warnings, even though they had witnessed God's miracles and had a long history of being God's chosen people. The more they sinned the farther they went from fellowship with God and the more stubborn they became.

Could God have forced his people to follow him? Could he have melted their hearts with the wave of a hand? Certainly. But

Dig Deeper:

"Stubborn" comes from the Hebrew word, *carar*, which translates to slide back. We usually think of a stubborn person as staying in one spot, but God sees that person as sliding backwards away from him.

his desire was to lead them gently into a closer relationship (pasture) and to spare them from any harsh punishments. Whenever our heels (the fleshy, callused part we walk on) are planted in stubbornness, we, like the Israelites, cannot be led. In addition, God cannot give us the good things he desires to give.

Background Bulb:

Animals are notorious for being ornery. We need animal trainers, shepherds, and handlers to herd and to teach them appropriate behaviors. In Hosea 4:16 God compares Israel to a stubborn heifer—a young cow who, being just barely over the age of one, will not budge. The nation of Israel experienced hardships as a result of sin. Warring tribes were allowed to overtake them; they wandered in the wilderness far longer than necessary and many died before entering the Promised Land of Canaan.

Weed & Water:

Stubbornness, when it takes hold in a person's heart, can lead to true rebellion. We can suffer consequences as the result of stubbornness. Friends may get mad at us, we hurt others deeply, or we may walk far away from God.

One of the best ways we can show our devotion to the Lord is by confessing sinful habits such as "digging in our heels" when we should be open to his plans for our lives. Through daily prayer we have the opportunity to guard our hearts, minds, and spirits against stubbornness. By doing so, we will slowly but surely begin to more closely resemble a gentle lamb.

Think about it:

Name two recent situations in which you might have been as stubborn as the Israelites or a toddler.

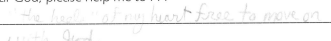

At workplace

At home

Which is more likely to please God, a tender heart or an unyielding one?

a tender heart

Prayer Pot:

Dear God, please help me to . . .

"the heels" of my heart free to move on with God.

Check the "heels" of your heart. They will either be stuck in the mud and mire or free to move on with God.

Love That Gray Hair

Today's Seed

> "Gray hair is a crown of splendor; it is attained by a righteous life."
>
> Proverbs 16:31

That first gray hair. What a shock!

In the backs of our minds, we knew it was coming, but we kept moving happily through life, acting as if it would never happen to us. Then that one morning comes along and there it is, shining from among its colorful siblings in all its glory. We may yank it out or begin the costly cover-up routine, but we can't ignore the inevitable.

The most important inevitability for us all is the moment our spiritual selves separate from our physical selves and come face-to-face with the Creator who will hold us accountable for how we have lived. And like dealing with that gray hair, we often try to excuse our lifestyle by yanking out the thought of dealing with it or covering up the sins that are choking the life we should be living. Gray hair attained by a righteous life is a splendor, an outward testament to a heart turned toward God. Live a righteous life and love that gray hair.

Dig Deeper:

The Bible considers gray hair to be a crown of glory. The Hebrew word for "glory" is *tipharah*, which means beauty, bravery, an ornament.

Background Bulb:

In biblical days, old people were revered because of their knowledge, experience, and wisdom. Older people were used by God to mentor younger people. Psalm 92:13–14 says, "Planted in the house of the Lord, they will flourish in the courts of our God. They will still bear fruit in old age, they will stay fresh and green." Old age was also seen as a reward for having lived a righteous, godly life. What a difference from the way in which many of our elder family members are viewed today!

Weed & Water:

We color our hair because we want to look younger. It may be OK to look younger, but it's not OK to act immature. A certain amount of wisdom should come with age, and knowing how to live righteously before God is an area where that wisdom should be evident. Examine your behavior. Do you have a mature, righteous lifestyle? Think about your spiritual growth. Settle down, and become comfortable with your age.

Think about it:

How do you feel about growing older?

Excitement, rewarding

In what areas would you like to act more mature or wise?

My age, My life

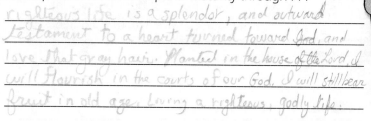

Prayer Pot:

Lord, help me to be an example of maturity through . . .

righteous life is a splendor, and outward
testament to a heart turned toward God, and
love that gray hair. Planted in the house of the Lord, I
will flourish in the courts of our God. I will still bear
fruit in old age, living a righteous, godly life.

"The glory of young [women] is their strength, gray hair the splendor of the old."

Proverbs 20:29

A Daughter Forever

Today's Seed

"He said to her, 'Daughter, your faith has healed you. Go in peace and be freed from your suffering.'"
Mark 5:34

Jesus rushed to heal a little girl who was dying. On his way a crowd mobbed him, and a woman who had been bleeding for twelve years reached out and touched his robe. Joy filled her heart as she was instantly healed. Jesus, knowing what just happened, stopped and to the confusion of the pressing crowd asked, "Who touched me?"

Why did Jesus stop?

The woman was healed, her greatest need met, and all her hopes and dreams of the past twelve years came true in that single touch.

Why did Jesus stop?

She didn't need the public humiliation—the scandal of an "unclean" woman touching a man. Surely this would do more harm than good.

Why *did* Jesus stop?

She fell at his feet and fearfully revealed the whole story. And he opened his mouth, not in rebuke, but in favor. "Daughter, your faith has healed you."

Dig Deeper:

The Greek word for "faith" is *pistis,* and is commonly used for a specific reliance on Christ. Jesus made it clear to this woman that it was her faith that brought forth the healing, and not some superstitious touching of his garment.

Daughter.

My child.

My precious one.

You belong. No more are you an outcast. No longer are you barred from worshiping in the temple, having a family, hugging your brother. Daughter, you are family once again.

Why did Jesus stop?

Because he knew that her greatest need was more than physical. Her greatest need was a spiritual welcome—a proclamation of her Savior that her Father claimed her as his own and called her by the precious title of "Daughter."

Background Bulb:

A specific condition made this woman ritually unclean. Therefore, she was excluded from most normal social relations. Anyone coming into contact with her also would be considered unclean and have to go through a rigorous cleansing process. This incurable illness ruined her life for twelve long years, until Jesus gave her new life in his name. Interestingly, Jesus went from here to give new life to a little girl who had died. The girl was twelve years old.

Weed & Water:

When dealing with socially difficult people, remind yourself that they, too, are daughters of God. Treat them accordingly. Find a way to encourage a struggling sister today. Write a note, give a call, meet for coffee, and tell her of God's fatherly love.

Think about it:

Think of a time when you felt like an outcast and needed to be accepted. What would have made you feel loved?

At home, my husband rejected me.
Turning to God, trusting Jesus,

How has Jesus shown you that you never need to be an outcast again?

Jesus gave me new life in his name,

What is one way you can remind yourself daily that you are God's beloved daughter?

God's fatherly love he made me,

Prayer Pot:

Thank you, Father, that I, too, am your daughter. Help me to take comfort in this when . . .

you need to.

I am a great daughter of the greatest Father!

Mighty Energy

Today's Seed

> "To this end I labor, struggling with all his energy, which so powerfully works in me."
>
> Colossians 1:29

Sometimes it seems as if the work we are trying to do for the Lord is really hard labor. This seed says it so succinctly: "struggling." And that is often where we stop. We agree we are laboring for the Lord, and it is a struggle. But wait, that is not where the seed stops. It goes on to say, "with all his energy, which so powerfully works in me." If what we are doing is really the Lord's work, then it isn't dependent on our strength.

Jesus taught us that he did nothing on his own. In John 14 he reminds us that all of his words and works are from the Father (God) working in and through him. He also said that he will send the Holy Spirit to live in us so that all we say and do will also be God's work through us. If the work we do "for the Lord" is a constant struggle, perhaps it is time to take a second look and see if our work is more our idea than his.

Dig Deeper:

The Greek word for "energy" is *energeia*. It means the power of God working to complete the task that has been given to us.

Weed & Water:

How many times have you said "yes" to a project that needed to be done, not because you felt called to do it, but because you felt guilty if you said "no"? God does not "need" us to accomplish his purposes on earth. However, God does give us the privilege of joining him in what he is doing. The difference is that we understand the work is the Lord's and our part is to join him. When we join in working with the Lord, we won't be "struggling." We will do it with a different attitude, not depending on our own strengths or talents. We will realize that if God has called us to work alongside him, he will also provide the energy we need to get the job done.

Sprout & Scatter:

Understanding that not every project put before us is our responsibility will give us an opportunity to seek out others who may be better suited for that job. The *Living Bible* paraphrases Colossians 1:29 this way: "This is my work, and I can only do it because Christ's mighty energy is at work within me." When God asks us to do a specific job, we will experience that energy. When we try to do a job that someone else is better suited to do, we short-change others and ourselves. In learning to share the work we not only lessen the burden on ourselves, but we also give others the chance to discover Christ's "mighty energy" at work within them.

Think about it:

What jobs might you be doing in your own strength rather than depending on Christ's mighty energy?

Wife, mother, associate, prep cook

What jobs are you doing that could be done by someone else?

Pizza dough, Sandwich maker, cleaning, Utility

Prayer Pot:

Dear God, help me to know when to . . .

work with you Lord, and help me to know when to work with you Lord along aside you, provide the energy to get the job done. Who do you want to share the work to do it lessen the burden or burdens on me. Thank you Lord.

Doing God's work won't wear you out.

Powerful Words

Today's Seed

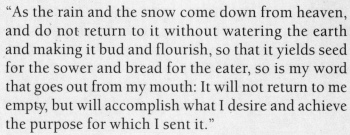

"As the rain and the snow come down from heaven, and do not return to it without watering the earth and making it bud and flourish, so that it yields seed for the sower and bread for the eater, so is my word that goes out from my mouth: It will not return to me empty, but will accomplish what I desire and achieve the purpose for which I sent it."

Isaiah 55:10–11

The day dawned slowly with the sun hidden behind low-lying clouds. Haze, so thick you could feel it, filled the early morning air with the promise, or threat, of rain within the hour. There go the plans to work in the garden today. We'll have to go to plan B.

We can't choose the weather. All we can do is accept it.

But not God. He controls the weather with the power of his words. The weather, like all things on earth, is controlled by the Word of God. He tells the snow to cover the earth and it does— two inches or two feet according to his decree. The same with rain. He sends a light shower or a downpour. The seed is watered and grows and gives grain for bread.

Dig Deeper:

The Hebrew word for "watering" means watering abundantly, soaking, making drunk, or satisfying to the full. God's Word will fill us abundantly.

God's voice equals power—power like humans know nothing about. But God doesn't keep his words for himself. He has shared his words. If we listen to them, we will accomplish what he has set out for us to do and more. God's Word offers insight into our daily life. It guides us and blesses us and creates a shelter for us when we need one. And God's Word also offers us the opportunity to grow, like plants after the rain.

Background Bulb:

Isaiah's prophecy that the Israelites would be released from their exile in Babylon continues in these verses and focuses on the reunion of God and his people. Isaiah describes how the people will be renewed and the Jewish homeland will again flourish to the point that the "hills will burst into song before you, and all the trees of the field will clap their hands" (55:12). All this is possible because the promise of God's Word is good and what he wants to accomplish will be done.

Sprout & Scatter:

Instead of trying to help or comfort others with our own fumbling words, we can remember to speak or write God's Words to those around us. Here's one idea to try: Choose a packet of flower or herb seeds from your favorite nursery. Plant them in rich soil, water them faithfully, give them enough light, and watch them grow. When they are sturdy and strong, repot them, attach today's seed, and give to friends and family.

Think about it:

When you open your heart to God's Word, what happens?

It guides me and blesses me.

Imagine yourself as a flourishing garden. What do you see?

Light, growing, sturdy, strong, powerful

Prayer Pot:

Lord, give me the right words—your powerful words—
to live by when I . . .

will accomplish what he has set out for me to do
to grow like plants after the rain. But Word will
he's fill us abundantly.

God's words have precious power.

Strangers in a Foreign Land

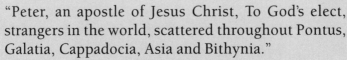

"Peter, an apostle of Jesus Christ, To God's elect, strangers in the world, scattered throughout Pontus, Galatia, Cappadocia, Asia and Bithynia."

1 Peter 1:1

Do you ever feel as if you are a nomad wandering in the desert? You find little creatures in the sand, birds in the air, and other nomads who speak a foreign language but no one who is just like you. You try to enjoy their company and they try to enjoy time with you, but sooner or later they all go off with their own kind.

As Christians living in this world we can feel like we don't belong. Our goals and actions don't match others. We feel like aliens. To make it worse, others may even snub us.

Peter wrote today's seed at the opening of his letter to believers scattered throughout the area that is now Asia Minor. Less than fifty years after he wrote these words, being a Christian in the Roman Empire became a punishable crime. Peter acknowledged the feelings of his readers and went on to remind them that they were residents of God's kingdom.

Dig Deeper:

The Greek word for "stranger" means a sojourner, an alien alongside, a resident foreigner, or a pilgrim. Our true country of origin is not earth but heaven.

We can take comfort from knowing that we are not alone in our occasional discomfort. Jesus was a sojourner or stranger in this world too. Imagine how uncomfortable it was for him, a man of perfection in a world of sin.

The good news is that this is a temporary home. Think of it as an interim move—like renting a temporary home while your new custom-designed home is being built! And soon, we'll be moving into a place where we will not be foreigners, but fellow citizens with God.

Weed & Water:

The next time you're feeling out of place, examine the circumstances. Perhaps you are doing or saying things that hurt others, making them keep their distance from you. If not, then you may just be feeling like the readers of Peter's letter. True Christians will have times when they feel out of place. Remember that you are just passing through earth on your way to your true home—heaven. You belong to God.

Sprout & Scatter:

We live in the melting pot of the world, which provides us a wonderful opportunity to reach out to foreigners. Scatter seeds of God's love. Start with the basics—guide them to the best schools, the best mechanic, dentist, dry cleaner, or grocer. Introduce them to neighbors, your church family, or others who will welcome them into your community.

Think about it:

Why do Christians sometimes feel like strangers in the world?

We Know this is not our place

Who can you help to belong?

People that love me.

Prayer Pot:

Father, when I feel like a stranger help me . . .

to move into a place where I would not be a foreigner, but fellow citizens with God.

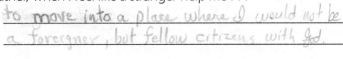

You belong to God and his country.

Sibling Rivalry

Today's Seed

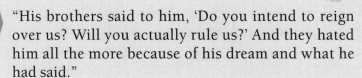

"His brothers said to him, 'Do you intend to reign over us? Will you actually rule us?' And they hated him all the more because of his dream and what he had said."

Genesis 37:8

Any parent knows that rivalry is to be expected among young sisters and brothers. Whether traveling together in the car, shopping, or simply playing a game—no amount of attempted fair attention will prevent the inevitable argument over who mom loves best. As children, we are jealous of any attention our siblings receive—we want it all! Sibling rivalry is rooted in jealousy.

The same was true of Joseph and his brothers. To make matters worse, their father actually did love Joseph more than the others. Being born late in Jacob's life, Joseph was a surprise blessing. His father showered him with special attention. But does that excuse the behavior of his brothers? They were adults when they schemed to get rid of Joseph. As adults, they were responsible for their actions.

Dig Deeper:

The Bible uses both "hate" and "envy" in telling the story of rivalry between Joseph and his brothers. When we hate we oppose, separate from, and have no desire for contact. The root of the Hebrew word for "envy" means to become very red because of high emotion—something we associate with anger and hatred.

Like Joseph's brothers, many of us carry our childhood jealousies into adulthood and feel justified—using past hurts as our excuse. When we carry childhood jealousy into adulthood, we risk using our children as pawns in our game of jealousy. As a result, we also risk polluting or contaminating their relationships with cousins and other family members. What a sorry legacy that is.

Jealousy is defined as a negative envy caused by a desire for something that rightly belongs to another. So, in fact, jealousy can also be defined as a desire to steal. Our jealousy robs or steals our children of the potential for a more loving and positive relationship with family members. How could we possibly find justification for that?

Background Bulb:

Jealousy has two sides: negative and positive. As a positive emotion, jealousy can mean full commitment or intense love. The Old Testament describes God as jealous. In this case the word is used in its positive sense. God deeply cares for his people. His commitment is emotional as well as decisive. As a loving, jealous God, he showered Israel with blessings.

Weed & Water:

Examine your life. Are you still carrying the baggage of childhood jealousy between you and a sibling? Admit your anger, stop the quarreling, and commit yourself to begin a positive, loving relationship with your sibling. We cannot change the past, but we can choose to move forward and make a positive difference in our lives and the lives of loved ones. By choosing to be a positive catalyst instead of an instigator of trouble, we can cause a positive response in others.

Think about it:

Examine your life for jealousy. How has this sin affected you and your family?

To help me or us move forward, a make
a positive decision in our lives

How would you feel if God told you that the thing you are jealous of in your sibling's life is a gift from God?

Alright.

Prayer Pot:

Father, help me to change my behavior to a positive jealousy when I feel . . .

you close to me.

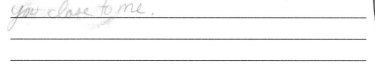

The Lord our God is a divinely jealous God.

Second Chances

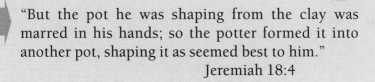

Today's Seed

"But the pot he was shaping from the clay was marred in his hands; so the potter formed it into another pot, shaping it as seemed best to him."
Jeremiah 18:4

Have you ever seen a potter working on a pot at the wheel? It is amazing to see how evenly and beautifully the clay takes shape. Sometimes the clay will contain a lump that ruins the shape of the pot as it spins. The potter doesn't throw the clay away. Instead, he stops the wheel, removes the hard lump, and begins again making a new clay pot.

The Bible is full of stories about people who were given a second chance. Instead of going to Ninevah, Jonah disobeyed God and got swallowed by a great fish. When he turned back to God, he got a second opportunity to go to Ninevah. David sinned greatly. When he confessed, God forgave him and allowed the throne of Judah to remain in his family line for generations. Peter was a loudmouth who acted on impulse and even denied that he knew Christ, yet he became one of the greatest preachers of the first century.

Dig Deeper:

The Hebrew word for "live" is *chayah,* which not only means to live but also to revive. It is often translated recover, repair, and restore. God is the giver of new life.

It is impossible for us to erase our actions, but it is possible to start over today. Every twenty-four hours God gives us a brand new start. Our job is to repent of our sins, forgive ourselves, and give God an opportunity to develop us.

Background Bulb:

A potter may work on a piece of clay for days before he puts it on the wheel. He will knead it, wet it, dry it, tear it apart, and put it together again. He may even put it on a shelf for a while. Through all of this, the clay becomes perfectly pliable. God will allow you to experience all sorts of ups and downs in your life. Then when his timing is right, he will form you into the person he wants you to be.

Sprout & Scatter:

It is easy to soften the impact of our failures by saying that we made an honest mistake. We like the appearance of being a good person who is just having a bad day. Remember that your family or friends may be having a bad day too, so it is important to give them the benefit of the doubt just as you would give yourself. Overlook those cutting remarks and get over it if they fail to call. Give them a second chance just like God gave you.

Think about it:

What failures and mistakes do you need to put behind you?

_____

_____

_____

How can you keep circumstances from ruining your attitude?

_____

_____

_____

Prayer Pot:

Lord, this morning I face a new day and I will start anew with you by . . .

_____

_____

_____

_____

_____

God is the God of second chances.

Renewed Strength

Today's Seed

> "But those who hope in the Lord will renew their strength. They will soar on wings like eagles; they will run and not grow weary, they will walk and not be faint."
>
> Isaiah 40:31

It's difficult to watch someone we love—husband, wife, mother, father, sister, brother, friend—weakened by disease. For some the weakness is from the illness that eats away at them; for others it's the treatment, the "cure," that saps their strength.

There's no way to take away the pain of illness. And no way a few words can take away misery, but faith in God can ease the pain.

Sometimes the culmination of an illness is death. If so, this seed can give hope and peace, an acceptance, a promise that even in death, if we hope in the Lord, we will soar as the eagles do.

Sometimes there is a cure, a recovery, and we or our loved one can rejoice in renewed strength, giving thanks to God who supports us. We can view today's seed as saying, "Don't be afraid! God's here and if you put your hope in him, he will give you strength."

Dig Deeper:

The Hebrew word for "soar," *alah*, is translated in a variety of ways, including to ascend, excel, or leap. God isn't stingy when he gives strength; he gives enough so we can rise high above the troubles.

The God who created the universe, hung the stars in place, and called them by name is the same God who cares for us. Like a shepherd, God gathers his people as if they are "lambs in his arms and carries them close to his heart; he gently leads those that have young" (Isaiah 40:11).

Background Bulb:

Today's seed was written to the Israelites in exile in Babylon. The exile of the people of Jerusalem began in 586 B.C. and ended nearly fifty years later in 538 B.C. The people were tired and prone to think that God felt as they did. They feared that he had forgotten them or didn't have the energy or will to rescue them. The words were intended to comfort and encourage them as the end of the exile neared.

Weed & Water:

Lean on this seed when you or someone you love is weak and weary. In fact, hold on to this seed at the end of every day—even when you're worn out with the stress of getting through the day. With God's help you can run and not be weary. Cling to those words. Share them with someone you love who needs to hear them.

Think about it:

Why do you think the prophet felt the need to write these words?

_____
_____

_____

How do you feel when you read the words "soar on wings like eagles"?

_____
_____

_____

Prayer Pot:

Lord, give me wings to fly above pain and illness . . .

_____
_____
_____
_____
_____
_____

The Word of God can lift you up and strengthen you.

Patience

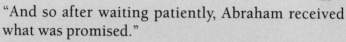

"And so after waiting patiently, Abraham received what was promised."

Hebrews 6:15

Waiting. Some days it seems as if that's all we do. We wait our turn to get into the shower. We wait to pay for our gas at the convenience store. We wait in traffic on our way to work. We wait for an important phone call. We wait for a loved one to return to God. We wait.

It's hard to wait patiently. The longer we have to wait, the harder it gets. Abraham is commended for waiting patiently to receive what God promised to give him. In Genesis 12 God promised to make Abraham into a great nation, to bless him, to make his name great, and to bless all people on earth through him. So Abraham waited. And waited. And waited. Abraham waited twenty-five years for God to start fulfilling these promises by giving him a son. That's right! Twenty-five years. And we mumble when we have to wait an extra ten minutes when we pick up the kids after school!

Dig Deeper:

The Greek word for "patiently" is *makrothumeo*, which means to suffer long or be longsuffering and not to give in to despondency. The word is used for being understanding toward people rather than things.

Abraham had no children when God first gave these promises, but the Bible says Abraham patiently waited for God's timing. Patience is a virtue, the saying goes. So Abraham was not only the most patient man in the Bible but also one of the most virtuous! How many of us could wait that long for a promise to be kept? Abraham had not only patience and virtue on his side. He also had faith in God and a certainty that God would keep his promise.

Background Bulb:

Although Abraham is congratulated for his faith, he didn't always get everything right. Genesis 15 and 16 records Abraham and Sarah's attempt to "help" God fulfill his promise to them. After ten years of waiting for Sarah to conceive, Abraham lay with his wife's maidservant, Hagar, and asked God to build his line through this son, Ishmael. For the next thirteen years Abraham didn't hear from God. Then in Genesis 17, God finally spoke but not to rebuke Abraham. God affirmed his original promise and told Abraham he would have a son through Sarah. As a sign of his promise, God began the rite of circumcision.

Weed & Water:

Impatience, despair, and doubt are temptations that may keep us from waiting patiently. Abraham and Sarah may have thought they misunderstood God's promise. We can learn from their mistake and go to God in prayer, asking for guidance before we try to "help" God fulfill his promises. If God is silent, do nothing and wait patiently. When God speaks, write down his promise and post it at a prominent place. Refer back to the promise often, especially during times of doubt or despair.

Think about it:

If you had been Abraham, what may have made it difficult for you to wait patiently?

_____

_____

_____

God viewed Abraham as patient despite his sin with Hagar. How does this help you?

_____

_____

_____

Prayer Pot:

Lord, help me resist despair and to wait patiently for . . .

_____

_____

_____

_____

_____

_____

"Waiting is still an occupation. It is not having anything to wait for that is terrible."

—Cesare Pavese, *Il Mestiere di Vivere*

Delightful Living

*Today's
Seed*

> "Delight yourself in the Lord and he will give you the desires of your heart."
>
> Psalm 37:4

Most of us are drawn to the second half of this seed: "He will give you the desires of your heart." What are the desires of your heart? Have you fully realized them? If not, why not?

God tells us here, very specifically, all we have to do is "delight ourselves in the Lord" and he will grant those desires. But what does it mean to "delight ourselves in the Lord"? Delight is a word that is tossed around. "I am delighted to meet you." "How was the meeting?" "Delightful!" We have removed the core essence of the word "delight" and made it into an automatic response, almost like answering "Fine" when asked, "How are you?"

We have also become so accustomed to not receiving the desires of our heart that we hardly know what it is we really want.

Is there any reason for the order of ideas presented in this seed? First, we are to delight ourselves in the Lord. This is a very specific instruction. Then, we will receive the desires of our heart.

Dig Deeper:

The dictionary says delight means to "take great pleasure, find extreme satisfaction." Paul says in Philippians 4:4: "Rejoice in the Lord always. I will say it again: Rejoice!" Paul is saying that delight means to rejoice in God more than in what he gives us.

Background Bulb:

Many times we wait until God gives us what we want and then we delight in him. It is easy to rejoice when things are going our way. But Paul teaches us that rejoicing or delighting in the Lord is not dependent on our circumstances. Paul rejoiced when he was in prison. His singing and praising the Lord actually brought about his release. When we put our focus in the right place God is free to do wonderful miracles in our lives.

Weed & Water:

When we delight and rejoice in God, we take great pleasure in God for who he is, not just what he does for us. Often lacking the desires of our heart makes it difficult for us to delight in the Lord. Our worries and fears may shift our focus off of God and onto our situation. If we commit those worries and fears to the Lord and trust him for resolution we can begin to find extreme satisfaction in him. To help with this, make the word "delight" into a simple acrostic. This will remind you that the secret to getting the desires of our hearts lies in Daily Everything Laid Into God's Hands Totally.

Think about it:

What are the desires of your heart?

_____

_____

What keeps you from having the desires of your heart?

_____

_____

How can you shift your focus from your desires to delighting in the Lord?

_____

_____

Prayer Pot:

Dear God, please help me to learn to . . .

_____

_____

_____

_____

_____

_____

Daily Everything Laid Into God's Hands Totally makes it easy to delight in the Lord.

Comfort in Weakness

> "In the same way, the Spirit helps us in our weakness. We do not know what we ought to pray for, but the Spirit himself intercedes for us with groans that words cannot express."
>
> Romans 8:26

Sometimes we are so overwhelmed with what's happening that we're too weary to lift our heads off our pillows in the morning. Those are times when we can't even find the words to pray. Whether it's divorce, infertility, terminal illness, or discouragement in our ability to cope with another day at work or at home with the kids, we're told to pray to God for help. But what if the words just won't come?

Paul knew that the Romans faced this question, as we do today. Our troubles weaken us, and we are so confused, upset, or agitated that we can't find words to describe our feelings. All we can do is cry, "Daddy! Father!"

Paul says, "Don't worry! The Holy Spirit will take care of you and the problem." The Holy Spirit helps us pray clearly even when we speak in groans and cries. He translates our feelings into

Dig Deeper:

The Greek word for "weakness" is *astheneia*, which means feebleness of the mind. Like the Romans, we're feeble, lacking strength in our lives and in our prayers.

words that he relays to God. While he's at it, he comforts us. When we pray for or about the wrong things, the Holy Spirit nudges us and teaches us what to pray. He breathes God's desires into us.

We have the relief of knowing that the Spirit prays according to God's will, and we put our trust in God that he will do what's best for our situation.

Weed & Water:

When we're in need of comfort for those times when we can't pray because we're overwhelmed with grief, we should forget about putting our wants and needs into the "right" words. Don't use this as an excuse for not praying. God knows what's in our hearts and minds. We can say, "God, I don't know what to say, what to pray." The Holy Spirit will speak for us.

Sprout & Scatter:

When those you love show weaknesses in destructive areas or have troubles that seem insurmountable to them and to you, ask the Holy Spirit to intercede for them. Groan before the Lord about the situation and trust that he will understand the feelings of your heart. Ask the Holy Spirit to teach you what to pray about the problem.

Think about it:

When have you felt too overwhelmed to pray? Did you pray anyway?

_____

_____

_____

List some things the Holy Spirit does for us when we are too weak to pray.

🐞 _____

🐞 _____

🐞 _____

Prayer Pot:

Dear Lord, thank you for the Holy Spirit. I'm groaning about . . .

_____

_____

_____

_____

_____

_____

God hears our groans and heartfelt sighs and knows what we need—without the words.

Leaning Hard

Today's Seed

> "Trust in the Lord and do good; dwell in the land, and enjoy safe pasture."
>
> Psalm 37:3

Throughout the Bible we are told to trust in the Lord. Have you ever stopped to ask yourself, "How do I trust in the Lord?" Interestingly enough, we find it easy to trust many things every day. We trust that the chair in which we sit is going to hold us. We trust that the food we eat will nourish us. But we find it difficult to trust in the Lord.

That may be because we have found, the hard way, that it is easier to trust things than it is to trust people. We get our disappointments with other people mixed up with our relationship with the Lord. Time and again we have been disappointed. Our expectations have not been realized. Sometimes even our expectations of what God would do have not come to pass. Our trust has been undermined—perhaps because we have misunderstood what God means when he asks us to trust him.

Dig Deeper:

Trust means to turn from independence to total dependence. It is taking God at his word. It is leaning hard on him and depending on him to be able to hold our weight.

Background Bulb:

In Mark 9:21–24, we read about the man who came to Jesus. His son was possessed by an evil spirit since childhood. The father pleaded with Jesus to help them if he could. Jesus responded, "Everything is possible for him who believes."

The boy's father cried out, "I do believe; help me overcome my unbelief!"

Doubts and unbelief aren't new. The disciples had tried to heal the boy but failed. So the man's faith had been tested. No doubt he had already done everything humanly possible to help his son. Jesus was his last resort. His faith was frail, but he did not give up.

Weed & Water:

It is easy to tell others to trust God. Why is it so hard for us? Fear often intervenes in our ability to trust—fear that God may not see things as we do or want what we want. We want to believe God's plans are best, but the enemy assaults us with doubts and fears.

First John 4:18, *Living Bible,* reminds us: "We need have no fear of someone who loves us perfectly; his perfect love for us eliminates all dread of what he might do to us. If we are afraid, it is for fear of what he might do to us and shows that we are not fully convinced that he really loves us." In the midst of doubts and fears, remember this man's actions and prayer: "I do believe; help me overcome my unbelief!"

Think about it:

What has happened in your past that keeps you from trusting God?

_____

_____

What do you fear about turning from independence to total dependence on God?

_____

_____

What can you do to lean hard, putting your total trust in God?

_____

_____

Prayer Pot:

Dear God, help me to understand your wonderful love for me and to trust you for . . .

_____

_____

_____

_____

Fear not! God can be trusted!

Our Plans Versus God's Purpose

Today's Seed

> "Many are the plans in a man's heart, but it is the Lord's purpose that prevails."
>
> Proverbs 19:21

Life, it's been said, is what happens when we're making other plans. Many of us are list makers, complete with date book, organizer, or digitized appointment calendars. We know how to plan ahead.

Let's see—five minutes to brush teeth, ten minutes to take out the dog, ten minutes to drop the kids off at school, thirty minutes of exercise. But then we can't find the toothpaste, the dog doesn't cooperate, and the children "remember" that today's the day they're supposed to bring in five dozen "homemade" cookies for a class party! We are not in control! We plan, but life intervenes. If we're smart, we'll allow God to guide us through our days and weeks.

Trusting in God should be our plan. God doesn't do things without a reason. He has a purpose, a plan for each of us. Allow him to put that plan in action. When we see the big picture, Ezekiel 14:23 says, "You will be consoled when you see their conduct and their actions, for you will know that I have done nothing in it without cause, declares the Sovereign Lord."

Dig Deeper:

The Hebrew word for people's "plans" means thoughts, imaginations, or intentions. In contrast, the word used for God's "purpose" means design, counsel, project, or wisdom. We imagine what we will do, but God designs the circumstances of our lives.

There are days when we plan and schedule but God says, "Nope! This is what will occur today." We need to be flexible, adaptable—not like a vase, which shatters into a thousand pieces when dropped. We should be like Play-Doh, which can be molded into any shape.

Background Bulb:

Proverbs emphasizes that we are not in control, repeatedly. Proverbs 16:1 says, "To man belong the plans of the heart, but from the Lord comes the reply of the tongue." Proverbs 16:9 says, "In his heart a man plans his course, but the Lord determines his steps." And Proverbs 20:24 says, "A man's steps are directed by the Lord. How then can anyone understand his own way?" Enough, we get the picture. God is in control!

Sprout & Scatter:

Buy some Play-Doh. Gather your children or borrow some from the neighborhood and play together, molding and shaping the dough. Take a few minutes to think about how God is molding and shaping you. Then tell the children a story to illustrate this.

Think about it:

Remember a time when your plans opposed God's plans. How did you feel?

_____

_____

_____

When God's purposes prevail in your life, describe the result.

_____

_____

_____

Prayer Pot:

Lord, when things don't work out the way I plan help me to . . .

_____

_____

_____

_____

_____

_____

Live one minute, one hour, one day at a time, according to God's purpose.

Valuables

Today's Seed

> "Then he said to them, 'Watch out! Be on your guard against all kinds of greed; a man's life does not consist in the abundance of his possessions.'"
>
> Luke 12:15

If you became independently wealthy, what would you do with the money? Would you travel, buy a big home, or retire on a Pacific island? Isn't it fun to dream about the possibilities? In the early morning, TV infomercials hawk the wares of someone who has struck it rich. Tragically, innocent fantasy becomes an obsession with millions of people who are desperately grasping for money and possessions.

Jesus understood human nature. He knew that our hearts would long for things of value, so he said that we should watch out for what's valuable and what's not. An antique ring that belonged to your grandmother may not have any value if appraised by a jeweler, but if she took it from her wrinkled fingers and placed it into your tiny girlish hand, no one could calculate its value to you.

Dig Deeper:

The Greek word for "life" is *zoe,* which not only means breathing and being alive but also means a genuine active and vigorous life.

Things will not delight our soul, satisfy its desires, supply its needs, nor last as long as it will last. The problem is that we can never find contentment in things because as soon as we obtain one thing, we long for another. Possessions will not prolong life, prevent tragedy, or heal illness. So do we tend to depend on possessions? God does not promise to give us the abundance of things. He promises abundance of life. So every person can be rich.

Weed & Water:

It is easy to get caught in the trap of grabbing for more and more. If we work so many hours that we don't see our family, we have lost sight of what's valuable. If we spend every extra dollar on new clothes and jewelry, we may have missed the joys of a simpler lifestyle. The best things in life cannot be counted. Think before you buy something new. Our motto should be "Don't get your values wrong."

Sprout & Scatter:

We can help our friends become more aware of the true worth of life by focusing on values rather than possessions. When conversations turn to shopping for expensive items, try talking about the needs of children's ministry at church. Instead of lunch at the most expensive restaurant in town, take a brown bag to the park and talk about your families. Invite friends to bring family pictures to a party. Share memories in place of expensive food and entertainment.

Think about it:

What possessions held great appeal to you until you realized they had no lasting value?

_____

_____

_____

How can you keep your desires in control?

_____

_____

_____

_____

Prayer Pot:

Lord, free me from the grasp of possessions and show me the value of . . .

_____

_____

_____

_____

_____

The best things in life are not things.

Pure in Heart

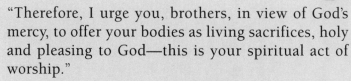

Today's Seed

"Therefore, I urge you, brothers, in view of God's mercy, to offer your bodies as living sacrifices, holy and pleasing to God—this is your spiritual act of worship."

Romans 12:1

When it comes to the Christian life, there is much confusion. We may ask, "Can I be a Christian and do this? Why shouldn't I do that? Other believers participate, why not me?" Sometimes we are truly confused; yet there are other times when in our hearts we know the right answer, but don't want to face it.

In these times what we are really asking is this: "How close to the edge of the cliff can I stand without falling over? How much of the world can I taste without losing my heavenly meals?" We are often tempted to leave the safety of the solid rock and begin to creep toward the cliff. Cliff-standing, or participating in "little" sins of this world, is tempting. We want to have the best of both worlds.

God's answer is always the same: "Holiness comes first—purity of the heart, purity of the soul, purity of the mind, and purity of

Dig Deeper:

The Greek word translated as "to offer" or "present" is *paristemi*, which means to give presently, bring before, stand aside, and yield completely.

the body. Do not engage in any activity that threatens your holiness. My way is worth the struggle."

We must change our thinking about the cliff. Instead of asking, "How near to the cliff can I be?" we must ask, "How near to the Lord can I be? How much can I imitate his life? What can I do to strengthen my faith?" Then we can present our lives to the Lord, holy and pleasing to God.

Cliff-standing is risky business. Let us cling to the solid Rock instead!

Background Bulb:

In contrast to the Old Testament's sacrificial system, we are urged to be living sacrifices. As our bodies are a temple for the Holy Spirit, everything we do is to be an expression of the work Christ has done in our lives. The offering of our lives is a sacred service and a beneficial one!

Weed & Water:

Offering our lives to God may sound simple, but in practice it is very difficult. The spirit may be willing, but the flesh is always weak! Set limits for yourself in areas that are hard for you and then ask someone to keep you accountable.

Think about it:

In what areas do you act like the world?

_____

_____

_____

Instead of asking, "How much can I get away with," what should you be asking?

_____

_____

_____

_____

Prayer Pot:

Lord, help me to steer clear of the cliffs in my life such as . . .

_____

_____

_____

_____

_____

_____

"Rock of Ages, cleft for me . . .
Let me hide myself in Thee."

Dealing with Grumblers

Today's Seed

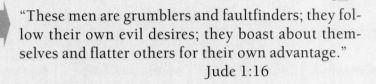

"These men are grumblers and faultfinders; they follow their own evil desires; they boast about themselves and flatter others for their own advantage."

Jude 1:16

Don't they just drive you crazy? Those grumblers we have to deal with day in and day out? Most of us don't live with a grumbler. (If you do, sorry.) But we all know what they're like. They see the glass as half empty, tell us about it, repeatedly, and then expect us to fill it for them.

Jude talks about the ungodly men, false teachers who corrupt the grace of God. They are concerned only with themselves and their wants and needs. They speak highly of themselves and flatter others if it suits their purposes. Jude explains that the grumblers and faultfinders are never happy.

People like this don't want to hear about logical solutions; they just want to grumble. Maybe they like the attention they get by complaining. Regardless of their motives, it helps to remember that they are unhappy people who need God's love and truth.

Dig Deeper:

The Greek word for complainers ("faultfinders") is *mempsimoiros,* which means blaming fate and being discontented. The more we complain and find fault, the more discontented we become.

Grumbling and faultfinding is contagious. One day we're sitting at work, minding our own business while our coworkers grumble. The next day we listen as they grumble and add fuel to one of their complaints. The following day we chime in a little more. Before we know it—we're grumblers too!

The good news is, we can guard against this "disease" with a healthy dose of God's Word and his son Jesus Christ in our lives. Our main responsibility is to keep a firm grasp on our own attitude and remain true to God.

Background Bulb:

Jude was eager to write about salvation but felt compelled to warn about the false teachers and grumblers who had already wormed their way into the body of believers. These teachers had corrupted the Christian message. They told believers that if they were saved by grace they could sin all they wanted since sin wouldn't be held against them. These men were thought to be forerunners of the second-century Gnostics.

Sprout & Scatter:

The next time grumblers or faultfinders take out their misery on you or someone you love, say a prayer that they might learn to know God and his healing ways. Respond to them in a cheerful manner, showing them the joy they are missing. If they believe untruths, try gently informing them of correct knowledge. If they accept your words, great! If not, keep your distance. Remember that we can't change them. Only God can change their hearts.

Think about it:

What were the false teachers teaching?

_____

_____

_____

When grumblers surround you, how can you stay positive?

_____

_____

_____

_____

Prayer Pot:

Lord, help me to avoid grumbling and finding fault with . . .

_____

_____

_____

_____

_____

_____

Stay away from grumblers and faultfinders.

Food and Drink

Today's Seed

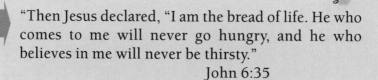

"Then Jesus declared, "I am the bread of life. He who comes to me will never go hungry, and he who believes in me will never be thirsty."

John 6:35

It's time to eat—again. Sometimes it's as if all we do is eat and drink. Breakfast, brunch, lunch, mid-afternoon snack, dinner, snack before bed, middle of the night munchies—we eat and eat. For some of us, it shows! Others munch and their metabolism keeps the weight off.

But the bread and drink that God offers provides so much more than mere nutrition or oral satisfaction. The bread of life Jesus speaks of is Jesus himself. When we come to him, Jesus offers eternal life to us—if we believe in him. Our spiritual hunger will be satisfied; our spiritual thirst will be quenched.

We don't need to wait until our next meal to have our spiritual needs met. Jesus will meet them all—right now. Talk about fast food! Anytime we want food for the soul we can reach for the Bible. It will stay with us and not leave us hungry.

Dig Deeper:

The Greek word for "bread" is *artos*. Bread is the staple in diets across the world. Jesus gives life to us, as bread provides life-giving nutrition.

Jesus is the Bread of Life. He is the one who gives us physical life and spiritual meaning. He gives the promise of life in heaven after physical death and the encouragement of spiritual refreshment for hard days on earth. From food we get the energy we need to do life's chores. From God and his Word we get the spiritual power we need to resist temptation and discouragement.

We need to go to Jesus each day for his abundant supply of our daily bread.

Background Bulb:

This statement is the first of seven that Jesus used that began with the words "I am." It is similar to the Old Testament statement when God said to Moses, "I Am Who I Am" (Exodus 3:14). God told Moses he wanted to be known by this name. When Jesus used the same phrase, "I am," he was in danger of being stoned by the Jewish leaders as a blasphemer. The Jews recognized Jesus' claim as a statement of his deity, and they rebelled against that claim. Jesus wanted his hearers to trust in him as a person, not just believe he was great because of all the miracles he did.

Sprout & Scatter:

Don't be hesitant or self-conscious about saying a blessing for your meals when dining out. Set an example for your children, family, and friends by having a prayer, complete with bowed heads. It only takes a minute to thank God for what he has provided for you.

Think about it:

When Jesus described himself as the bread of life, what did he mean?

_____

_____

How does physical hunger compare to spiritual hunger?

_____

_____

If you were truly hungry spiritually, what would you do differently?

_____

_____

Prayer Pot:

Lord, help me to hunger and thirst for you by . . .

_____

_____

_____

_____

_____

_____

Jesus is food for the soul.

Exposing Your Heart

Today's Seed

> "For the word of God is living and active. Sharper than any double-edged sword, it penetrates even to dividing soul and spirit, joints and marrow; it judges the thoughts and attitudes of the heart."
>
> Hebrews 4:12

Visit any showcase of homes, and you will see beautiful decorations. Underneath the gorgeous cloth-covered tables by the bed you might find stacks of apple crates.

Like tablecloths that hide ugly crates, our appearances often hide our true thoughts, intentions, and attitudes. We may cover them up and make others think we are good Christians. We may even convince ourselves that we are not so bad, but God isn't deceived. He knows our insincerity, unbelief, and hypocrisy. His Word pulls back our beautiful facades to expose the crates in our hearts—crates filled with unethical behavior, long-forgotten sins, selfish motives, and unbelief.

God has no trouble seeing our weaknesses, but we do. God's Word is the tool that corrects our vision. How does it work? When we read a verse or chapter of the Bible, the "living and

Dig Deeper:
The Greet word *logos* is translated "word" in our English Bible. *Logos* means words, speech, or communication. God transmits his truth to us by the use of words.

active" words shine a bright light into the dark corners of our hearts. The light penetrates into the deepest crevices. It reveals the secret passions, appetites, and intentions that we keep hidden away. But it does more than reveal; it awakens us to the need for change. Once awakened, we are faced with the question: "Will I make the change?"

Weed & Water:

The sword of God's Word pierces into the control center of our hearts and divides the good from the bad. It is then up to us to get rid of the bad and keep the good. The only way to do this is to ask God for his help. Bad habits don't change overnight, and we may need to repeatedly ask God for help to change. He will always come to our rescue. He may use a sermon, a song, a friend, or the Bible to guide us to freedom.

Sprout & Scatter:

There are so many different Bible translations and para-phrases available today, including special Bibles for teens, men, and women. Think of a needy person and give them a Bible. If your friend is not open to receiving a Bible, try presenting them with a Christian book that has ministered to you. Just be sure the book you choose contains Scripture quotes.

Think about it:

How has the Word of God judged your thoughts and attitudes?

_____

_____

_____

What has God revealed that needs correction?

_____

_____

_____

_____

Prayer Pot:

Lord, please show me the contents of my heart and change . . .

_____

_____

_____

_____

_____

_____

Keep your heart in the right direction, and you won't have to worry about your feet.

A Purpose for Your Life

Today's Seed

> "Brothers, I do not consider myself yet to have taken hold of it. But one thing I do: Forgetting what is behind and straining toward what is ahead, I press on toward the goal to win the prize for which God has called me heavenward in Christ Jesus."
>
> Philippians 3:13–14

It's easy to get distracted these days. Life is so busy that most of us barely have time to think about our next move, let alone find the opportunity to look at the big picture. We get so wrapped up in daily details that we forget about our life's purpose. But that's no excuse. In writing to the church in Philippi, Paul instructed the believers to forget about past failures and excuses and to move forward, with their eye on the goal, focusing on the purpose God had called them to.

Some of us may not have defined our life goal or purpose—that can really make the job of staying focused a tough one!

God has designed each of us with a specific purpose in mind. Our talents, character, and personalities were crafted exactly for that one purpose.

Dig Deeper:

The Greek word translated "straining toward" implies continued repeated action done by the person acting upon him or herself. We have to take the initiative to find and continually live out the purpose God has for us.

Having a God-directed life purpose can give meaning to the seemingly unrelated or nonsensical events of our life. God is the architect of our lives. Each event, experience, and situation is designed to equip us for the work he has planned. To fall victim to life's hard times instead of pressing on toward the goal is to miss the prize of the higher calling of God. We are to leave behind the old baggage, shed the clutter, and run the race with single-minded discipline to claim all our inheritance.

Background Bulb:

It is thought that of all the letters Paul wrote to the churches, this one stands out as being the most personal. The concept of all-sufficiency of Christ is found throughout. And Christ gives meaning to life and causes people to serve him even to their death. How's that for a life purpose?

Weed & Water:

Having a life verse can be a good place to begin your life purpose statement. Ask the Holy Spirit to guide you in discovering your personal life verse or passage. It can become your life statement and be of great assurance that you are working according to God's plan. Consider writing a life purpose statement to help you focus on the big picture. Here's an example of one woman's purpose statement based on Romans 15:4: "I will be an encourager and bring hope to others."

Think about it:

If your child or other relative came to you feeling as though life had no purpose, how would you respond?

_____

_____

_____

Have you allowed the past to deny you the joy of pursuing your passions and life goals?

_____

_____

_____

Prayer Pot:

Father, show me your purpose for my life even in the midst of . . .

_____

_____

_____

_____

_____

Propose to know your purpose for life.

Set One Day Apart

Today's Seed

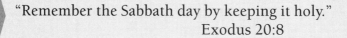

"Remember the Sabbath day by keeping it holy."
Exodus 20:8

The lawn needs to be mowed, the pantry shelves are bare, the kitchen floor needs to be mopped, and the dog needs to have a bath. But it's Sunday. What do we do?

Keeping the Sabbath as a day of rest is difficult. Despite all the "time-saving conveniences" we live with, there never seems to be enough time. With full-time jobs, part-time work, volunteer activities, church events, kids, family, and just "stuff" there's not enough time to do all we think we have to do.

"To reclaim (the Sabbath), you have to think, you have to plan. You're going to have to take God into your calculations," said Rev. Rusty Hedges, a United Methodist minister who challenged his congregation to make the Sabbath a day of rest. Do no chores, he told them. But it's not a day to do nothing.

Jesus emphasized that God's purpose for the Sabbath was to provide spiritual rest and mental refreshment. Jesus didn't care about all the rules the religious leaders had made. He said, "The

Dig Deeper:

The Hebrew word for "Sabbath" is *shabbath*, which means to celebrate, to rest, to keep an intermission. Celebrating the Sabbath provides a much-needed intermission in our lives.

Sabbath was made for man, not man for the Sabbath" (Mark 2:27).

When we give the Sabbath back to God, we should be prepared for a renewal in our spiritual life, a peace that allows us to think and plan. We'll have time not just to react to what's happening around us, but time to make God a part of our day. And once we use the Sabbath as it was intended, who knows what will happen. Only God knows.

Background Bulb:

God spoke the words of today's seed to Moses in the Ten Commandments, Israel's divine law. Of all the wonderful things God created, only the Sabbath was hallowed, made sacred, and set apart for God. God rested on the seventh day following creation and expects us to rest every seventh day too. After Jesus' time on earth, the early Christians met for fellowship on Sundays—the day Jesus rose from the dead. Most Christians now think of Sunday as their Sabbath.

Sprout & Scatter:

This Sunday give the entire day over to God and to freedom from work. Gather friends and family into God's plan of rest one day a week. You don't have to lie around all day and be bored. Attend a worship service, and then plan an enjoyable gathering. Play board games inside if it's cold or raining, croquet (remember that family game?) or badminton on the lawn if it's nice. Just make sure you share your day of rest with those you love.

Think about it:

What makes your Sabbath holy?

_____

_____

What might God want you to give up in order to keep the Sabbath holy?

_____

_____

How can you keep your mind from running through your list of things to do?

_____

_____

Prayer Pot:

Lord, help me accept the gift of a day of rest from . . .

_____

_____

_____

_____

_____

_____

Reclaim the Sabbath for God—and rest for yourself.

True Beauty

Today's Seed

> "Charm is deceptive, and beauty is fleeting; but a woman who fears the Lord is to be praised."
>
> Proverbs 31:30

Many women struggle with a "baby belly" after the birth of a child. We glance at ourselves in the mirror daily with determination to someday fit into our "real" jeans again. Our husbands can say we look beautiful. Friends can rave about our appearance; yet despite the compliments of others, we often view ourselves as overweight and unattractive.

In the search for beauty, we find many promises of hope—in the local gym, wild fad diets, expensive cosmetics, and hip fashions. We'll try them all. But each one leaves us feeling disillusioned and empty.

In Proverbs, God shows us the true beauty of a woman. It is not a size 8 waist and perfect hips. Beauty is found in our fear of the Lord. All our weight loss solutions do is keep us from the very scary prospect of inner evaluation. Distracted by the pursuit of outward perfection, we miss our needs within.

Dig Deeper:

The Greek word for "praised" is *halal,* which means to cause to shine and glorify. A woman who fears the Lord will be praised in this way! Others will say things about her that cause her to shine.

Beauty comes from knowing that we are God's children, with a worth beyond measure. As we seek God, we will be transformed into his likeness, reflecting the character of God Almighty.

While there is nothing wrong with losing your baby weight, place your value on inner beauty, the beauty of the Magnificent One shining through a life connected to him.

Godly character is the true secret of beauty.

Background Bulb:

Godly fear is the virtue that begins, ends, and fills the Book of Proverbs. All the attributes Proverbs extols as meaningful are represented by the woman in chapter 31. These qualities lead to praise, honor, worth, and enjoyment of life.

Weed & Water:

Time spent with our Lord is the most important time spent all day. In order to keep the balance between striving for outward beauty and reflecting God's inward beauty, it's a good idea to spend at least as much time seeking God as you do putting on your makeup.

Think about it:

What do you think you would gain by being more attractive physically? Spiritually?

_____

_____

_____

How do you gauge your value? How should you?

_____

_____

_____

_____

Prayer Pot:

Father, let your beauty shine through me today when I . . .

_____

_____

_____

_____

_____

_____

"If you are ugly at 16, it's not your fault. If you are ugly at 90, it is."
—Unknown

Facing Difficulties

Today's
Seed

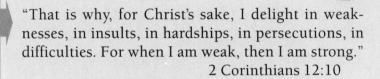

"That is why, for Christ's sake, I delight in weaknesses, in insults, in hardships, in persecutions, in difficulties. For when I am weak, then I am strong."

2 Corinthians 12:10

Have you ever been on one of those jungle boat rides at an amusement park? As you travel through the jungle, the alligators almost catch the boat. The pirates threaten but are scared away at the last moment. From the shore a cannon fires, but the shell lands just short of the boat. No matter how many times you take that ride, you will always come out safely. The cannon shot will never hit the boat. The arrows will always whiz by. There is never any real danger.

But there are real dangers and difficulties in the Christian life. You will be pressured. You will be laughed at. You will be isolated. But God will never abandon you. He will always keep you safe.

The benefits of difficulties are hard to imagine while we face troubles, but the Christian never loses. Christ turns our negatives to positives. He turns weakness to strength. He turns fear to peace. He uses the dangers we face to develop loveliness of char-

Dig Deeper:

Paul said *when I am weak, then I am strong*. The Greek word for "when" is *hotan*. It means as soon as. Trusting in Christ is instantly depending on him the moment that the difficulty arises.

acter in us. The arrows and cannons of life cannot harm us because God is using each dangerous or unpleasant situation to strengthen us.

Background Bulb:

Paul's declaration of dependence on God is part of a letter that he wrote describing all the things he had been through since he became a Christian. His experiences found in chapters 11 and 12 were frightening and amazing. He had faced every kind of danger, but he had also seen the power of God in his life. He came to the conclusion that whatever came into his life was not to harm him but to make him better.

Weed & Water:

When Paul said that he delighted in weakness, insults, and difficulties, he didn't mean that he enjoyed pain and ridicule. The delight he felt was in the way he was able to handle problems in Christ. He was glad that the problems were going to change him from his old way. When we know that God is going to make us better or stronger, we will discover that we can embrace the difficulties that we face.

Think about it:

What difficult event of your life has ultimately made you better?

_____

_____

_____

What weakness of yours has God turned to strength?

_____

_____

_____

_____

Prayer Pot:

Lord, today please help me face everything with your power . . .

_____

_____

_____

_____

_____

_____

The difficulties of life are intended to make us better—not bitter.

Your Testimony

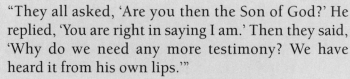

"They all asked, 'Are you then the Son of God?' He replied, 'You are right in saying I am.' Then they said, 'Why do we need any more testimony? We have heard it from his own lips.'"

Luke 22:70–71

What if you were on trial for being a Christian? Imagine the courtroom scene. Picture the jury, the judge, the attorneys, the witnesses, the bailiff, the onlookers, and yourself. Witness after witness is grilled by the attorneys—all in an effort to prove your "guilt." Are you a Christian? Would the things you do and say condemn you or set you free?

Jesus was put on trial for claiming to be who he was. The religious leaders asked. He answered. What else could he say? He said he was God because that's who he was, and he was condemned to die.

If we live the Christian life as the Bible instructs, we too run the risk of persecution and condemnation. In fact, if we are so bold as to live out our faith in public, the Bible actually promises us trouble. (See Matthew 5:10–12, 25.)

Dig Deeper:

The Greek word for "testimony" means a declaration that both informs and corroborates the testimony of a witness. Your testimony certifies that you say you are a Christian and corroborates the testimony borne out in the Word of God.

Frankly, we are on trial every day. Once people know we are Christians, the jig is up. They are checking us out to see if there's enough evidence to convict us. Has the jury reached a verdict in your case?

Background Bulb:

The fact that Jesus was convicted on his own testimony at his Jewish trial is only one of the many illegal things that were done to condemn him. The testimonies of two or three witnesses had to agree against a criminal, the trial must take place in the daytime, a quorum of twenty-three judges was necessary, and a guilty verdict could not be rendered until the following day. At Jesus' trial, the witnesses couldn't agree, it was night, there was no quorum, and the guilty verdict was rendered on the spot because of Jesus' own words.

Weed & Water:

It is always good to be mindful of whether or not what we do and say lines up with God's standards. Make it a point this week to evaluate at least one response you make to someone each day. Make sure that response is a testimony of who you are as God's child.

Think about it:

What have you done or said recently that would have caused a non-Christian to doubt your testimony?

_____

_____

_____

What have you done or said recently that caused others to know you were a Christian?

_____

_____

_____

Prayer Pot:

Lord, let others see your love in my life as I . . .

_____

_____

_____

_____

_____

_____

If you were on trial for being a Christian, would there be enough evidence to convict you?

Planning a Quiet Place

Today's Seed

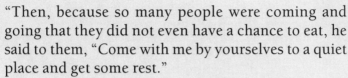

"Then, because so many people were coming and going that they did not even have a chance to eat, he said to them, "Come with me by yourselves to a quiet place and get some rest."

Mark 6:31

One mother of three admitted that she wants her epitaph to read "All she wanted was to go to the bathroom in peace." Not having time to eat doesn't bother her, if only she could have five minutes alone in the bathroom.

A quiet place. Even if we are not raising three children, we long for a quiet place. Somewhere to dream, to think, to rest, to do nothing. We're surrounded by sounds and people most of the day. We can't get away from the noise unless we plan time away.

Jesus was quick to realize that there was too much going on for his apostles to have time to eat. They needed a quiet place. But like us, they couldn't get away from the hullabaloo. A large crowd followed them everywhere they went. They needed an escape, and Jesus had a plan.

Dig Deeper:

The Greek word for "come" is *deute,* which means to follow. We need to follow Jesus' example of finding a quiet place to think and to pray.

Jesus sought a quiet place regularly. The key is, he sought the quiet. It didn't come on its own. "Very early in the morning, while it was still dark, Jesus got up, left the house and went off to a solitary place, where he prayed" (Mark 1:35). "After he had dismissed them [the disciples], he went up on a mountainside by himself to pray" (Matthew 14:23).

Jesus knew the value of quiet time for his disciples. We need to learn the value of quiet too. If the only place you can get away from it all is the bathroom, go for it. If everyone follows you to the bathroom, head for the hills.

Weed & Water:

Don't feel guilty about taking time for yourself. Guilt comes from Satan, not God. God wants you to feel the healing power of rest. Start with just five or ten minutes. The world—and your family—will survive without you! Lock yourself in the bathroom. Or get up while it's still dark, and sit on your porch. Take time to breathe in the fresh morning air. Take a short walk in the evening after the kids are in bed. Use the time to quiet your mind. Don't think about what you have to do next. Focus on God's creation and his love for you.

Sprout & Scatter:

Encourage each family member to find a quiet place alone at a certain time each day. No TV, no video games, no CDs — just a quiet time to rest, read, or think. Take the phone off the hook, or put on the answering machine. Set a timer so small children will know when "quiet time" is over. Enjoy!

Think about it:

How can you commit to spending five minutes a day in a quiet place?

_____

_____

_____

List the quiet places you've found.

_____

_____

_____

_____

Prayer Pot:

Lord, help me discover a quiet place in my life by . . .

_____

_____

_____

_____

_____

_____

Make time to find a quiet place.

Never Alone

Today's Seed

> "While they were still talking about this, Jesus himself stood among them and said to them, 'Peace be with you.'"
>
> Luke 24:36

When we were young, we didn't want our parents always looking over our shoulders. We were either afraid they'd spoil all our fun or we wanted to do something we figured they'd disapprove of, so we struggled for our independence. It was a fate worse than death to have your mother accompany you to the door of the party and ask to meet the chaperone.

Some of us achieved the independence we sought sooner than others, but we eventually all found out the same thing—independence wasn't all it was cracked up to be. We had to wash our own dishes and clothes, pick up after ourselves, drag ourselves out of bed and head to a job day after day, and use our own hard earned money to pay taxes and bills.

The funny thing is, as we become mature Christians, we become more and more aware of the need for our Father to look over our shoulders. In fact, the exciting thing is that we have

Dig Deeper:

The Greek word for "among" is *mesos,* meaning middle. What a comfort to know that God is in the center of our lives—"rubbing elbows" with us.

the Holy Spirit ever in our midst since he lives within our hearts.

Background Bulb:

Today's seed was spoken after Jesus' resurrection. Before Jesus was crucified and resurrected, the disciples had hoped that Jesus would deliver Israel from Roman rule and establish an earthly kingdom. After Jesus' death all their hopes were dashed. They felt abandoned. As they discussed the events of the previous days, Jesus suddenly appeared among them, talked to them, touched them, and ate with them.

Jesus was seen five times on the day he arose. He was first seen by Mary Magdalene and then by the women who were on their way to tell the disciples that he was alive. Next, Peter saw Jesus, and then he appeared to the two disciples who were traveling to Emmaus. Finally, Jesus was seen by the eleven disciples at once.

Weed & Water:

Are you facing some challenges in which you are struggling to steer clear of sin? Get up each day, and remember that the Holy Spirit is actually going to be *with* you everywhere you go all day long. Wear a special necklace, ring, or lapel pin that you designate as your reminder of his presence.

Because the Holy Spirit is with you, he will guide you in knowing what to do or say. He will strengthen you to resist temptation. Send up a prayer for help, and imagine Jesus being at your elbow wherever you go.

Think about it:

What makes you feel alone as if God has abandoned you?

_____

_____

_____

Who can you depend on to remind you of God's love and presence, "rubbing elbows" with you?

_____

_____

_____

Prayer Pot:

Lord, thank you for being with me when . . .

_____

_____

_____

_____

_____

_____

God rubs elbows with everyone through you by being in you.

Seeking Approval

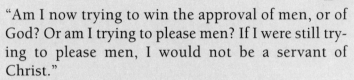

"Am I now trying to win the approval of men, or of God? Or am I trying to please men? If I were still trying to please men, I would not be a servant of Christ."

Galatians 1:10

It's great to have lots of friends. We all like to be liked. The problem we often run into is the temptation to change so that others will like us or to avoid their anger. We become chameleons to gain the approval of others.

Being flexible is great—up to a point. But there are times when we should hold fast to our beliefs regardless of whether or not we will make others angry. We might win the approval of our children if we never discipline them, but that would not be to their long-term benefit. We might be the most popular person at work if we spent our days telling jokes and forwarding funny e-mail lists, but that would not benefit our careers or our companies.

Paul was not a politician. He didn't care if what he had to say displeased his audience. This letter to the Galatians was written to correct errors in their thinking. Some people were saying that

Dig Deeper:

The tense of the Greek word for "please," *aresko,* refers to continuous repeated action, not a once and done thing. Trying to please people is an ongoing struggle; the target always moves.

faith in Christ wasn't enough for salvation and for holy living. These people taught that followers of Christ must live by all the Old Testament laws, including circumcision and other rules related to the Jewish lifestyle. These teachers also attacked Paul, saying he wasn't an apostle and that he was giving people a license to sin.

Paul knew that the people of Galatia were no different from people everywhere—we often give in to please others so they won't be angry with us. Paul said the Galatians should follow the Holy Spirit's guidance and look to God for approval.

Background Bulb:

Paul tells the Galatians that they should be more Christlike and be filled with love, joy, peace, longsuffering, gentleness, goodness, faith, meekness, and temperance. These are also known as the fruit of the spirit. Paul admonished the Galatians to walk, work, and live in God's ways, not the ways of the people around them. We, too, need to turn away from seeking the approval of others and live the way God wants us to live. Be assured that with God's approval, we don't need the approval of others.

Weed & Water:

Sometimes we just can't help it. We want the approval of others. We think we *need* the approval of others. What we really need is to focus on God's Word. Write today's Bible seed on a slip of paper and tape it on your bathroom mirror so that you see it each morning and evening when you brush your teeth. Take a good look at yourself. Discover where you are looking for approval.

Think about it:

How far will you go to gain approval of others?

_____

_____

_____

_____

How far will you go to gain approval from God?

_____

_____

_____

_____

Prayer Pot:

Lord, help me to look to you for approval when . . .

_____

_____

_____

_____

_____

_____

Approval should come from God, not man.

Debt of Love

Today's Seed

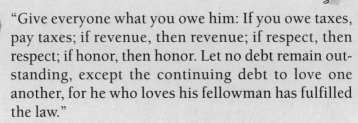

"Give everyone what you owe him: If you owe taxes, pay taxes; if revenue, then revenue; if respect, then respect; if honor, then honor. Let no debt remain outstanding, except the continuing debt to love one another, for he who loves his fellowman has fulfilled the law."

Romans 13:7–8

Some of us dread the arrival of the mail. Those envelopes with windows mean that another bill has arrived.

The Bible's way of dealing with debt is simple. If you owe someone money, pay it back! There is one debt, however, that Paul encourages. In fact, he says, let it continue! That's our debt to love one another. It may feel strange to consider that loving one another could be called a debt. When writing to the Romans from Corinth on what was probably his third missionary journey, Paul wanted them to feel the obligation to love one another. He also made clear that they should love their fellowman, according to the Mosaic law, which set down moral and social responsibilities.

Dig Deeper:

The Greek word for "owe" is *opheilo,* which means to be indebted and to be bound. It implies moral obligation and personal responsibility.

The basis for our debt of love to others is the debt relief Christ granted us by saving us. We owe Christ—are in debt to Christ—for his all-encompassing love for us. The only proper response to Christ's love is to love others the way he has loved us.

Since Christ's love for us will always be more than what we mortals can produce, we will be continually in debt. But being in debt to Christ carries no fear of a cancelled account. Christ's love for us is unending.

Weed & Water:

Sometimes—perhaps a lot of time—it's not easy to love our fellowman or woman as Paul encouraged. Some people are just not very lovable. Or maybe we're the ones who have a hard time letting down our guard and allowing others into our lives. But, according to God's Word, we have this debt to pay. Loving one another is the only way it can be paid. So, take it one person at a time.

Sprout & Scatter:

Love for fellow Christians and people in general is central to God's law. Just as we make sure we pay our bills, we can open our hearts to those around us. There are many ways. Volunteer at church, in a soup kitchen, or at a youth organization. Give both time and money to a worthwhile charity. When driving, we can wave a driver to enter traffic in front of us, hoping that driver will pass our goodwill on to others.

Think about it:

To whom do you owe a debt of respect or honor?

_____

_____

_____

_____

How can you take the first steps in following the law to love one another?

_____

_____

_____

_____

Prayer Pot:

Lord, help me to pay my debt to others by . . .

_____

_____

_____

_____

_____

Be debt free, except the debt to love one another.

Choices

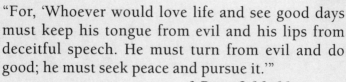

Today's Seed

"For, 'Whoever would love life and see good days must keep his tongue from evil and his lips from deceitful speech. He must turn from evil and do good; he must seek peace and pursue it.'"

1 Peter 3:10–11

Imagine that you are on a plane finally taking your dream trip to Hawaii. Your bags are packed with summer outfits and sandals in every color, but as the plane lands you notice snow on the ground. When the cabin door opens, the air is icy cold. Just then the flight attendant says, "Welcome to the Alps!"

If that happened to you, you would be faced with a choice—either cry and complain that your trip is ruined or head for the nearest ski shop and get outfitted for the most beautiful snow in the world.

Our lives consist of choices. We decide every morning what kind of day it will be. Peter says if we want a life worth loving and want to see good days, we must make some careful choices. The first choice is what to do with our tongue and lips. Peter suggests keeping away from evil and deceitful speech. This means that our word choices must be good, not evil, and focused on truth, not

Dig Deeper:

One of the meanings of the Greek word *thelo,* which is translated "will" in today's seed, is intend. We can live and love life on purpose—intentionally.

deception. It means that we should not whisper behind someone's back or say unkind things even in a joking sense. We make the choice to control what comes out of our mouths.

Peter doesn't limit his advice to our tongue; he points to our actions too. "Do good," he says. Don't give lip service only. Actually *do* something good.

Weed & Water:

Solomon struggled with the opposite view of life. He said, "So I hated life, because the work that is done under the sun was grievous to me . . . " (Ecclesiastes 2:17). Solomon had tried wine, fun, possessions, power, friends, sex, hobbies, money, and awards, but none of it made him love life. Peter's view is that loving life is an act of the will. We don't need possessions and accolades to make life great. We don't need long life to make life worth loving. We only need to make our choice. Will we choose good not evil?

Sprout & Scatter:

Our attitude about life will spread to those around us. If we complain, grumble, and find fault, they will too. If we look for the positive, we can change the mood of a meeting or conversation. If we choose the good, the bad will seem unimportant. Our positive influence will sway others. How do we keep a positive attitude? By remembering our joy in Christ Jesus. If we allow it, his joy will overflow from our lives to others.

Think about it:

What event has kept you from loving life?

_____

_____

_____

Will you make a choice now as an act of your will to discard that bad memory?

_____

_____

_____

_____

Prayer Pot:

Lord, help me choose joy today when . . .

_____

_____

_____

_____

_____

_____

In a difficult situation, choose joy.

Leadership

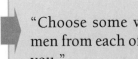

Today's Seed

> "Choose some wise, understanding and respected men from each of your tribes, and I will set them over you."
>
> Deuteronomy 1:13

Overhead a huge flock of birds dips and swirls, turning the sky gray with flapping wings and soaring bodies. How do they know where they're going? Why don't they run into each other? Who is in charge here?

When God created birds he gave them an innate sense of space. Maybe God also gave them an innate sense of who among them should lead.

One of the first things that Moses did when the Israelites were camped along the Jordan River ready to enter the Promised Land was to appoint leaders.

What makes a good leader? Moses listed three qualities: wisdom, understanding, and respect. This is a little different from the criteria for the leaders of today, isn't it? Too often good looks, popularity, and money—lots of money—make today's leaders rise to the top.

Dig Deeper:

The Hebrew word for "understanding," *bin,* not only means to discern and perceive, but also to be intelligent and to teach. God wants leaders who are understanding and can pass their knowledge on to others.

Moses needed to set up leaders. He couldn't do everything himself. He needed help to bear the people's problems, burdens, and disputes. We, too, need someone to guide us. But they need to be good leaders. In Moses' case, he had the people choose from among each of the tribes the best people to help in the day-to-day job of governing. Moses then appointed the leaders to their tasks, some over large groups of people and others over small groups. Such division of labor helped to spread out the responsibility and to train younger people to take over as leaders aged.

Weed & Water:

When we are called to be leaders, we need to follow Moses' example and find assistants to help us. It's easy to decide—now that we're in charge—that we know best and that everything should be done exactly the way we would do it. It's easy to forget wisdom and understanding when we're in authority. But if we want to continue to command respect from those we lead, we need to remember to listen and to perceive the needs of those we lead. Leaders are not called to satisfy their own needs but to serve others.

Sprout & Scatter:

Look for the qualities of wisdom, understanding, and respect in those you elect to positions in your church, community organizations, and local, state, and federal positions. When you know a person is a good leader, spread the word to others.

Think about it:

What do you look for in a leader?

_____

_____

_____

_____

When you are in a leadership position, what qualities
do you think you need?

_____

_____

_____

Prayer Pot:

Lord, give me what it takes to be a leader—and a follower . . .

_____

_____

_____

_____

_____

_____

Follow good leaders, and lead by
following God.

Wise Words

Today's Seed

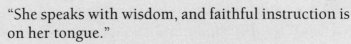

"She speaks with wisdom, and faithful instruction is on her tongue."

Proverbs 31:26

Don't you wish people would say that about you? Sometimes we don't know the right thing to say, but even more often, we blurt out the *wrong* thing.

We should be like David, who wrote, "I will watch my ways and keep my tongue from sin; I will put a muzzle on my mouth . . ." (Psalm 39:1). Have you ever wished you had a muzzle for yourself? We all have times when we should just be quiet. David, too, had problems controlling his tongue. In Psalm 39 he wrestled with wanting to speak and wanting to be silent. He didn't want anyone to misunderstand his words.

When we don't have muzzles, we can consider how our listeners might interpret our words. If we think before we speak, we'll have the satisfaction of knowing that what we've said is what we meant. We also need to be aware of our body language and our tone of voice. Sometimes lifting our eyebrows or folding our arms can speak louder than our words.

Dig Deeper:

The Greek word for "wisdom" is *chokmah*, which means skillful, wisely, and with wit. Humor can be a part of wisdom.

The "virtuous woman" mentioned in Proverbs 31 had things under control—including her tongue. She knew who she was. From other verses in this chapter we know she didn't pretend to be someone she was not. She also shared faithful instruction with others. We've all learned a lot in life, and we can enjoy sharing our knowledge if we do it the right way at the right time. Doing that takes wisdom. If we follow the advice of the woman in Proverbs 31, we won't need muzzles.

Background Bulb:

Proverbs chapters 30 and 31 were written by someone other than Solomon. Both chapters are called prophecies. Chapter 31 is a poem with twenty-two verses, each beginning with a successive letter of the Hebrew alphabet. The chapter lists all the attributes that godly women should have. It does *not* describe one specific superwoman. What a relief!

Weed & Water:

The words we use can be powerful—they can cause harm or they can heal. What we say and how we say it affects others. Everyone loves a woman whose mouth speaks words of blessing and comfort rather than harsh commands. A touch of humor can soften even hard-to-deliver truth.

Think about it:

What do wisdom and faithful instruction have in common?

_____

_____

Think of a time when you held your tongue. How do you think it changed the outcome of the situation?

_____

_____

What are some ways you can avoid the common habit of speaking more carefully to others than to your family?

_____

_____

Prayer Pot:

Dear Lord, give me the grace to speak with wisdom about . . .

_____

_____

_____

_____

"It's better to keep one's mouth shut and be thought a fool than to open it and resolve all doubt."
—Abraham Lincoln

Sweet Sleep

Today's
Seed

"The sleep of a laborer is sweet, whether he eats little or much, but the abundance of a rich man permits him no sleep."

Ecclesiastes 5:12

Experts say we need seven to eight hours of sleep each night. For many of us, that's impossible. A full-time job, a full-time family, church activities, school events, sports, workouts, crafts, and hobbies take time—time that we rob from our sleep time. Then when we go to bed, we have trouble falling asleep or staying asleep. We might get by if only we could sleep soundly.

Often what keeps us awake are worries over money or how to maintain the things we have. We're told in Ecclesiastes that when we're too concerned about money and possessions, especially acquiring more, we'll find ourselves embroiled in anxiety which leads to sleepless nights and exhausting days.

In contrast to the warning about riches in this seed, there is a blessing to hard work—peaceful sleep. The person who works at a physically demanding job sleeps well because he or she is exhausted. Hard work and exercise enable us to sleep well—even if we have only seven hours to spend in bed.

Dig Deeper:
The Hebrew word for "sleep" means to give in to our exhaustion. It can also mean to be slack or slow, without energy.

Background Bulb:

Solomon, thought by many scholars to be the author of Ecclesiastes, sought an anchor for his lost spirituality near the end of his life. He wrote Ecclesiastes to search for the meaning of life. After accumulating amazing riches, pleasures, and worldly successes, Solomon came to one conclusion: "'Meaningless! Meaningless!' Says the Teacher. 'Utterly meaningless! Everything is meaningless'" (Ecclesiastes 1:2). The more possessions we have, the less we *really* have. Through God's grace we have all we need—salvation and a relationship with him.

Weed & Water:

Are you living beyond your means? When we've allowed money and possessions to take over our lives and we toss and turn trying to figure out how to get more, more, more, that's a sign that we are out of balance. Consider ways to simplify your life. Halt spending, and start saving. Cut down on activities that aren't necessary. Learn to say no. Ask God to show you what is most important. When we turn to God instead of possessions, this blessing will be ours: "When you lie down, you will not be afraid; when you lie down, your sleep will be sweet" (Proverbs 3:24).

Think about it:

How can possessions keep a person too busy to focus on Christ?

_____

_____

What possessions or desires are calling you away from Christ?

_____

_____

What changes do you need to make?

_____

_____

Prayer Pot:

Lord, show me what has true meaning in my life . . .

_____

_____

_____

_____

_____

_____

The one who dies with the most toys still dies!

God's Word

Today's Seed

"The precepts of the Lord are right, giving joy to the heart. The commands of the Lord are radiant, giving light to the eyes."

Psalm 19:8

Martha Stewart often gives a hint for better living, which she calls good things. It is fun to listen to her and consider doing something unusual that would brighten our home or make us smile. But the really good thing of life is not a household hint; it is the Bible that sits on our table.

The person who experiences the greatest blessings is the one who has a love affair with God's Word. No other activity will bring us such strength and joy. When God's Word is on our mind and in our heart at all times in every situation, we experience true happiness.

The pages of our Bible are full of delightful things. Intriguing stories, love stories, poetry, and history are woven throughout the book. Reading it is a delight. Our pleasure is multiplied when we realize that as we read it we learn what to do, what to treasure, and how to please God. Discovering these added bonuses puts the

Dig Deeper:

The Hebrew word for "right" is *yshaariym*. It means to make smooth. The Bible is like a guide who knows the most straight and safe path to take. We aren't left to find our own way.

light in our eyes that the psalmist mentions. It is the "good thing" that brightens our life and puts a smile on our face.

Background Bulb:

In the New Testament, Luke tells about one day in the life of Jesus when a woman in the crowd approached him. She said that it must be wonderful for his mother to have such a son. Jesus agreed that his mother was blessed. In fact, he agreed that all mothers are blessed. Then he said, "Blessed rather are those who hear the word of God and obey it" (Luke 11:28). Jesus knew that even motherhood does not compare with the joy of knowing the Word of God.

Weed & Water:

Experts agree that it only takes a few weeks to develop a habit. Mark your calendar and make a commitment to read your Bible every day for the next twenty-one days. The habit will then be a part of your life. You can start by looking up each day's seed and reading the surrounding passage. As you read the Bible pick out a verse that gives you joy or contains an instruction. Write the verse on a small card. Each time you see the card, thank God for his blessings or ask him to help you obey the instruction.

Think about it:

Name some verses in the Bible that give you a feeling of joy.

_____

_____

_____

When will you begin your new habit of regular Bible reading?

_____

_____

_____

Prayer Pot:

Lord, help me find true happiness in your Word. I'll start today by . . .

_____

_____

_____

_____

_____

A Bible that is worn and falling apart from use usually belongs to someone who isn't.

A Well-Watered Garden

Today's Seed

> "The Lord will guide you always; he will satisfy your needs in a sun-scorched land and will strengthen your frame. You will be like a well-watered garden, like a spring whose waters never fail."
>
> Isaiah 58:11

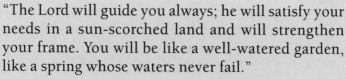

Some summers are wet and gardens flourish. Other years, rain showers are few and far between. Without water, gardens wilt, then wither, and finally turn a dry, crisp brown. Flowers, plants, and trees die without life-giving water.

Without spiritual water, we wilt too. When stumbling blocks and boulders are part of our lives, the efforts to overcome them sap our strength and we become like a garden without water. We look bad, and we feel worse. But one of God's miracles is that a garden that looks dead will revive when consistent watering begins again. We can be revived too.

Jesus offers us living water to satisfy our spiritual needs. Like the well-watered garden that blooms, we too will flourish when we depend on Jesus. We can turn our problems over to him, saying, "Lord, I need your help."

Dig Deeper:

The Hebrew word for "guide" is *nachah,* which means to lead, as in leading troops into battle or leading sheep to water. Jesus will lead us when we've lost our way and are searching for life-giving water.

We'll discover how he can quench our thirst and answer our needs. By drawing on his strength through prayer and Bible reading, we'll develop strong spiritual roots capable of withstanding dry spells and boulders. And, like a spring that waters a lush garden, we'll have the resources to spread God's love by watering others.

Background Bulb:

Isaiah's 66 chapters are divided into two sections: chapters 1 through 39 are words of judgment, while chapters 40 through 66 are words of comfort. The image of water is used throughout the whole book. Isaiah 55:1 is an invitation to come to the Lord: "Come, all you who are thirsty, come to the waters." Those who do are promised complete satisfaction and forgiveness from sin: "Let him turn to the Lord, and he will have mercy on him, and to our God, for he will freely pardon" (Isaiah 55:7).

Sprout & Scatter:

The lessons we have learned and the verses we have found helpful during dry times are the same ones that we can share with others who are hurting. Look around. Is there someone you know who needs spiritual "watering?" The words of the Lord are the water that can nourish them, but we can be the watering can to bring help. Send a thinking-of-you card and include a verse of Scripture. Deliver a plate of cookies, bunch of flowers, or jar of jam with a note saying you are praying for them. Visit a shut-in and read aloud from Scripture. If you have musical talent, play or sing some favorite hymns to nourish them.

Think about it:

Think back to the last time you were dry and thirsty. What verse nourished you?

_____

_____

_____

When you encounter difficulty, what do you do first?

_____

_____

_____

_____

Prayer Pot:

Dear Lord, guide me and satisfy my needs for . . .

_____

_____

_____

_____

_____

_____

The source of strength is living water—God.

Contentment

> "I am not saying this because I am in need, for I have learned to be content whatever the circumstances."
>
> Philippians 4:11

Contentment is the state of being content, of bringing peace or quiet to our desires. This definition just barely skims the surface. The kind of contentment we're talking about is the contented cow version—they don't desire much, just plenty of green grass. Some of us are like cows; we're happy just doing what we're doing, chewing our cud (or a piece of gum), and watching the world go by.

Others among us need a bit more to be content. A good book, a cup of Darjeeling tea, and an uninterrupted hour or so to relax. Others feel contented when they are busy writing or researching, knee-deep in a topic that removes them from the present. Still others need to immerse themselves in nature—hiking a scenic mountain trail, skiing down a snow-covered mountain slope, or floating in a raft on a crystal-clear stream.

But these types of contentment are fleeting. True contentment needs to be constant in our lives, not moments that interrupt our discontent. Paul knew how to be content whether he had enough

Dig Deeper:

The Greek word for "content" is *autarkes,* which means satisfied, as Paul was content and deeply satisfied with his life with Christ.

or nothing. He relied on Christ to supply whatever he needed, not in a physical sense, but spiritually. He says, "I know what it is to be in need, and I know what it is to have plenty. I have learned the secret of being content in any and every situation, whether well fed or hungry, whether living in plenty or in want. I can do everything through him who gives me strength" (Philippians 4:12–13).

With confidence Paul assures the Philippians that whatever the future holds, he will be content because God will meet his needs. Can we say that with any confidence?

Background Bulb:

Paul was in prison when he wrote these words. He had hoped to receive a gift from the Philippians. Prisoners in Bible times were usually responsible to supply their own food and clothing, so not receiving a hoped-for gift would have been a blow to Paul. But he is careful to reassure his readers that he can get by with the things he has. He doesn't want them to feel bad.

Weed & Water:

Paul looked to what he could *do* to be content, not on what he should *have*. Sometimes our lack of contentment comes from emptiness inside. Examine yourself to see if the emptiness you're feeling is because you, unlike Paul, are not relying on Christ for strength. Perhaps you are expecting too much in the way of material goods. Ungratefulness can also rob us of contentment. The Bible tells us to be thankful in all things.

Think about it:

How does Paul's example of contentment help you today?

_____

_____

_____

For what are you thankful? List your blessings here.

_____

_____

_____

_____

Prayer Pot:

Lord, forgive my ungratefulness and grant me a spirit of contentment about . . .

_____

_____

_____

_____

_____

Contentment is being thankful for what we have.

What's Due?

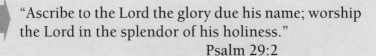

"Ascribe to the Lord the glory due his name; worship the Lord in the splendor of his holiness."

Psalm 29:2

A humorous bumper sticker that is a takeoff of a popular Disney movie song reads, "I owe, I owe, so off to work I go." It's funny, but it's so true. Except for those of us who are independently wealthy, most of us can sing the same song. If we're homemakers, we can sing it while we scour for bargains at garage sales and discount stores. The high cost of daily living sends us out of our doors or to our home office desks because something is due.

We all need a place to live, transportation, and food. But we can get so wrapped up in the struggle to pay what's due that we start pushing aside what's due to God.

Today's seed reminds us to give the Lord the glory due his name. And giving God that due glory is done by living a holy life—a life that is pleasing to him. Living in holiness is not a chore but a splendor. Living holy is a form of worship, and that's what's due.

Dig Deeper:

The word "due" was added to this seed by the translators of the Bible for better readability in English. This word is not actually in the Hebrew text. Without it, the text reads, "Give unto the Lord the glory his name . . ." It is then understood that the glory God's name gets is a high glory meant only for him. We live holy lives not for ourselves, but because of him.

Background Bulb:

The sanctuary in the Old Testament, the place where God and the people met, was a beautiful place. It was full of gold and rich tapestries. In the same way, our lives—the place where God meets us—should be beautiful, spiritually adorned with gold and tapestries, as we live holy lives to his glory.

Weed & Water:

Understand that holiness has to do with both attitude and action. Change your focus from struggling with the rightness or wrongness of each individual action and start concentrating on having an overall determination to live right in general. Once your mind is made up to please God, your actions will follow.

Think about it:

Do you honestly want to please God?

_____

_____

What habits do you have or actions do you perform that are not pleasing to God?

_____

_____

What do you plan to do about those habits or actions?

_____

_____

Prayer Pot:

Lord, I will give you the glory due to your name by . . .

_____

_____

_____

_____

_____

_____

"He who receives a benefit with gratitude repays the first installment on his debt."

—Lucius Annaeus Seneca,
from *On Benefits*

Facing Death

Today's Seed

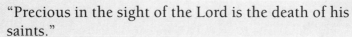

"Precious in the sight of the Lord is the death of his saints."

Psalm 116:15

We don't want to talk about it. We don't want to think about it. But death is part of life. Sooner or later the death of a loved one forces us to face death—up close and personal. As we get older, we're touched by death again and again—a parent, a dear friend, a spouse, or even a son or daughter. Death plays no favorites. It comes to all of us. "Death is the destiny of every man" (Ecclesiastes 7:2).

When a loved one dies—either slowly or suddenly—we may be angry and strike out at God and feel that God has abandoned us. In this dark time we need to hear the words of the psalmist who tells us that there can be joy in death. Joy in death? How can this be possible, we ask through our tears?

The answer? As death draws nearer, so does God. Death comes in God's time, and God watches over each of us and knows when we will need him most. The Bible assures us that when loved ones die, they are precious to God—as precious to him as they are to us.

Dig Deeper:

The Hebrew word for "precious" is *yaqar*, which means valuable. God puts a high value on each of us. Precious also means "carefully watched over." It's comforting to know that we are carefully watched over by God.

The good news for believers is that when *we* reach eternity—God will wipe every tear from our eyes. "There will be no more death or mourning or crying or pain, for the old order of things has passed away" (Revelation 21:4).

Background Bulb:

Psalm 116 is part of what has been called the Egyptian Hallel psalms (Psalms 113–118). They were used in worship at Passover when Jews remembered their slavery in Egypt and God's deliverance. The psalms were recited or sung before or after the special meal. Before Jesus and the disciples left the upper room to spend the night in the Garden of Gethsemane, they sang the Hallel. Perhaps Jesus was thinking of his own death as he sang these words.

Weed & Water:

When someone close to us dies, we're consumed by a myriad of feelings—anger, loss, and sometimes guilt. We may have left things unsaid and undone. Our loved one may have left things unsaid and undone. We might be angry that our prayers of healing were not answered the way we wanted. We feel our loss keenly. In the midst of our tears, we can know that God is with us, sharing our feelings and providing hope.

Think about it:

What words come to mind when you think of death?

_____

_____

_____

How does knowing that your loved one is precious to God help you?

_____

_____

_____

_____

Prayer Pot:

Lord, I'm glad we are precious in your sight. Carefully watch over . . .

_____

_____

_____

_____

_____

When death is near, God is nearer.

Be Squeaky Clean

Today's Seed

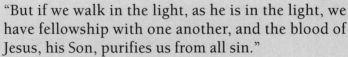

"But if we walk in the light, as he is in the light, we have fellowship with one another, and the blood of Jesus, his Son, purifies us from all sin."

1 John 1:7

Good smelling soap and a hot bath. What could feel better? We can have clean, fragrant bodies thanks to all today's great beauty products. But no one sells a product to clean us from sin.

Jesus came to earth to address this problem of inner filth. Sin entered the world through Adam and Eve in the Garden of Eden. God knew that a perfect sacrifice would need to be offered to take away the sins of the world. His Son, Jesus, became that perfect sacrifice because only his blood can remove the inner filth that pollutes our very nature.

Sin will not be removed by washing with soap and water. No matter how hard we try to clean up the inner man, only Christ's blood has everlasting power to cleanse us from within. Two thousand years may have passed since Christ's birth, death, and resurrection but his cleansing blood still purifies the human soul.

Dig Deeper:

This act of cleansing through Jesus' blood is a principle known as purification. The word "purify" is derived from *katharizo,* which means to clean, make free from filth, and in spiritual terms to clean from the pollution and guilt of sin.

Background Bulb:

In the Old Testament, people were required to bring animals to the priests to be sacrificed for their sins. The animals' blood only covered their sins; it did not take them away. So the people had to keep making sacrifices. Once a year the High Priest entered the innermost room of the tabernacle or temple, called the Most Holy Place, to sprinkle blood on the altar and to seek forgiveness, first for his own sins and then for the corporate sins of the nation. In addition to bringing sacrifices, the Jewish people also had to follow many other rules.

Weed & Water:

Old habits and sins are hard to break. Sometimes we find ourselves behaving in ways that even make us cringe. We know that Christ's love has reached down to us, but we mess up because we are human. Purification is an ongoing process. Sins, like dirt, need to be confessed and removed every day. The next time you pick up a bar of good smelling soap reflect on how much "soap" it takes to clean up the "dirt" that you cannot see. Ask the Holy Spirit to reveal a speck here and a speck there.

Think about it:

What areas cause you to sin or to disappoint God?

_____

_____

_____

How willing are you to allow his cleansing blood to work in those areas?

_____

_____

_____

_____

Prayer Pot:

Lord, cleanse and purify my heart of . . .

_____

_____

_____

_____

_____

_____

You are washed in the blood of the Almighty.

Attitudes Can Influence

Today's Seed

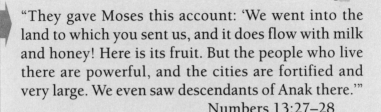

"They gave Moses this account: 'We went into the land to which you sent us, and it does flow with milk and honey! Here is its fruit. But the people who live there are powerful, and the cities are fortified and very large. We even saw descendants of Anak there.'"

Numbers 13:27–28

In a Bible study group several years ago, the women were told that they were the barometers of the family. The mood of the family would fluctuate up or down, depending on what kind of a day the woman of the house was having. Like the popular saying, "If momma ain't happy, ain't nobody happy!"

Our negative attitude affects our families—in a negative way. A bad attitude can even prevent us from receiving the good things that God wants to give us.

Sometimes our attitude is affected by situations that we don't feel able to handle. That was what happened when Moses sent scouts, or spies, to explore the land of Canaan. A leader from each tribe was sent to discover just what this Promised Land looked like. When they returned they said to Moses, "Do you want the good news or the bad news?"

Dig Deeper:

The Hebrew word for "land" is *erets*, which means a country—this time a particular land, the Promised Land.

The good news was that the land was wonderful. It flowed with milk and honey, meaning not that it was full of dairy cattle and beehives, but that the land was fertile. The bad news was that the people living there scared them. They were huge, powerful, and lived in walled cities. What should have been a joyful recounting of the goodness of the land was offset by the Israelite scouts' fearful and negative attitude.

Their negative opinions and exaggerations spread throughout the tribes and infected the rest of the people. Their fears colored their attitude and kept them from the good things God had planned for them.

Background Bulb:

The Promised Land was small, only about one hundred fifty miles long and sixty miles wide. God had promised this land to Abraham, saying, "To your descendants I give this land, from the river of Egypt to the great river, the Euphrates—the land of the Kenites, Kenizzites, Kadmonites, Hittites, Perizzites, Rephaites, Amorites, Canaanites, Girgashites and Jebusites" (Genesis 15:18–21). The Israelites should have marched in and taken the land, trusting God to win the battles for them. They should have relied on God's power to enable them to create a home there for themselves and their families.

Sprout & Scatter:

Your attitude can color your entire life . . . and the lives of others. Your children learn how to deal with things by your example. Set a good example! Watch how you report on events, knowing that what you say may sway others' opinions and feelings. Trust God, remember his promises, and be positive!

Think about it:

If you had been one of the Israelites, how would you have felt after hearing the scouts' report?

_____

_____

What promises of God have you been afraid to claim?

_____

_____

_____

_____

Prayer Pot:

Dear Lord, I confess my negative attitude about . . .

_____

_____

_____

_____

_____

_____

Change negative attitudes to positive ones by trusting God for the future.

Rest

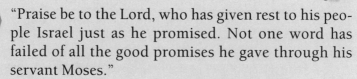

"Praise be to the Lord, who has given rest to his people Israel just as he promised. Not one word has failed of all the good promises he gave through his servant Moses."

1 Kings 8:56

After a long trip, sleeping in your own bed is a great delight. While beds in hotels or in friends' and relatives' homes may be clean and comfortable, nothing compares to settling into the familiar softness of your own pillow. Your body and mind both sigh when you finally lie down.

God has promised that we can rest in him. His rest means more than relaxing tired muscles. His rest gives peace and security to the soul. The satisfaction and serenity found in the rest of God cannot be duplicated, even on your favorite pillow.

How do you enter the rest of God? His rest is found in the simple act of believing him. God promised Israel a new homeland. But "they were not able to enter, because of their unbelief" (Hebrews 3:19). So for forty years the Israelites wandered aimlessly in the desert while the land that God had promised was

Dig Deeper:

The word for "promised" is the Hebrew word *dabar*, which means arranged. We can embrace the arrangements that God makes because he is trustworthy.

only a few miles away. If they had believed God would keep his promise, they could have gone to their new homes much sooner.

The Bible contains over eight thousand promises. God has never broken one of them. He never will. When we believe God, we rest because we believe that he is able and willing to keep those promises.

Background Bulb:

This seed is part of a speech Solomon made on the day that the new temple was dedicated. Solomon was one of the richest men who ever lived. Yet when he stood before the crowd that day, he didn't say anything about the wealth, fame, and power that he had accumulated. Instead, he said that the thing to praise God for was rest. God has never failed. We can count on it.

Weed & Water:

One of the best ways to increase your ability to believe God and allow yourself to rest in him is to remember how he has been faithful to you in the past. Think of a crisis time when you asked God to help you and remember how he came through for you. Remembering his blessings, guidance, and protection will help you trust in him no matter what happens today.

Think about it:

When has one of God's promises come true for you?

_____

_____

_____

How can you use his past faithfulness to build your faith now?

_____

_____

_____

_____

Prayer Pot:

Lord, when I begin to doubt, help me remember how faithful you were when you . . .

_____

_____

_____

_____

_____

Unbelief says, "God, you can't handle this one!"

God's Call

Today's Seed

> "Then I heard the voice of the Lord saying, 'Whom shall I send? And who will go for us?' And I said, 'Here am I. Send me!'"
>
> Isaiah 6:8

When you dream, ponder, and plan, do your plans include God?

Your answer is probably, "Sometimes." The calling of God seems like such a lofty thing. We think the phrase could apply only to a dignified minister or an amazing Mother Teresa–like saint. To be called of God appears much too grand for ordinary women with ordinary skills and backgrounds. Yet God calls each one of us to a special project for him. He sets his plan in motion from our birth through our childhood, adolescence, and adult years by equipping us with talents and abilities. Then he puts the opportunities in front of us so that we can go down the path he has planned for us.

When God called Isaiah saying, "Whom shall I send?" he wasn't asking for anyone's advice about which person to choose. Rather he was asking if anyone had the courage to accept the call. Most of us have calculated our own plan. We have figured and sketched

Dig Deeper:
The Hebrew word translated "send" is *shalach*, which means to stretch. When God calls, he may ask us to stretch in directions we've never been before.

exactly what we think we can do for God with little regard for what he may want. If we had Isaiah's kind of courage, we would say, "Here am I. Send me!"

Background Bulb:

Before Isaiah said yes to God's call, he had a vision. In fact, he joined a heavenly worship service in progress. God was seated on his throne high and exalted. The angels were calling out words of praise: "Holy, holy, holy is the Lord Almighty; the whole earth is full of his glory" (Isaiah 6:3). Isaiah was in awe of God because the vision made him aware of the magnificence and the power of the ruler of the universe.

Weed & Water:

When Isaiah saw God, he immediately saw himself and he didn't like what he saw. He said, "Woe is me!" The bright light of God's holiness penetrated into Isaiah's life, exposing all his sin. He felt unworthy to be in God's presence. He especially felt ashamed of his lips and things he had said. Seeing ourselves as God sees us is often the first way that God gets us ready for his call.

Think about it:

What past events have prepared you for God's plan for you?

_____

_____

_____

How is God calling you to serve him now?

_____

_____

_____

_____

Prayer Pot:

Lord, I pray for your purpose not mine in . . .

_____

_____

_____

_____

_____

_____

To be brought into the zone of the call of God is to be profoundly altered.

Lasting Memorials

Today's Seed

> "I tell you the truth, wherever the gospel is preached throughout the world, what she has done will also be told, in memory of her."
>
> Mark 14:9

A memorial service is held in honor of a person who has gone on before us. We associate memorials with grief, death, burials, or tributes to fallen soldiers. Plaques and statues are erected to honor special citizens. But did you know that living memorials exist today?

Your words, actions, and deeds will not go unnoticed. Friends and family members will continue to reflect on your life and the contributions you made. By living a life that is pleasing to God, you are in essence leaving some sort of mark or memorial for future generations, whether you realize it or not. The circle of our influence is endless.

Jesus associated with people from all levels of society. He did not separate himself from those in lowly positions. In fact, his closest friends were fishermen, tax collectors, ordinary women, and even prostitutes. Mary, the sister of Martha and Lazarus, is an example of an ordinary person who left behind a godly heritage.

Dig Deeper:

The word translated "memory" in English means a reminder, memorial, or record. Mary's actions left a visible picture in the hearts of those who knew her best and on those who now read of her devotion. This memorial has been handed to us in Scripture.

One day Jesus attended a dinner at the home of Simon at Bethany. We know from John 12:3 that Mary, sister of Martha and Lazarus, was there. Mary decided to demonstrate her love for Jesus. After opening an expensive jar of aromatic oil, she anointed his head with the fragrant oil. The disciples and those seated beside Jesus scoffed. "How could she *waste* this perfume?" they yelled.

The others could not understand her actions. Her goal was to please her master. And in this way, she left a godly memorial.

Background Bulb:

This account of Mary anointing Jesus' head is recorded twice in the New Testament, here in Mark and in Matthew 26:13. The two sisters were considered something of a hospitality team because Jesus was a frequent visitor to their house. Jesus had predicted his death, and it is thought that Mary took this news to heart. Perhaps this is why she chose to pour her perfume, often used in embalming, on Jesus while he was still alive.

Sprout & Scatter:

Because Mary acted out of sincerity and not "showiness," Jesus mentioned her as one whose name would be referred to again and again. Each day we can take opportunities to leave living memorials. Can you nurture your children or parents through the lesson of Mary's life? If we live out our faith in a humble, consistent manner before others, we may never be honored with a plaque that says, "Dynamic Woman of the Year." But God sees our legacy. Make it your goal to be an example.

Think about it:

Imagine yourself doing what Mary did. What would be the result?

_____

_____

List two persons who have their memorials in your life and write a note about them.

_____

_____

Describe a portion of the legacy or memorial you are leaving.

_____

_____

Prayer Pot:

Dear Lord, help me to leave behind . . .

_____

_____

_____

_____

_____

Only you can determine the kind of memorial you will leave behind.

Friendship

Today's Seed

> "Two are better than one, because they have a good return for their work: If one falls down, his friend can help him up. But pity the man who falls and has no one to help him up! Also, if two lie down together, they will keep warm. But how can one keep warm alone? Though one may be overpowered, two can defend themselves. A cord of three strands is not quickly broken."
>
> Ecclesiastes 4:9–12

In an Iroquois story, passed down through the generations, maize (corn), beans, and squash are spoken of as the three sisters. These important vegetables were the mainstays of the Iroquois diet and, when planted together in their gardens, supported each other. The tall corn stalks supported pole beans and the squash vines on the ground suppressed weeds and kept the soil moist.

Too many times in our lives, when we need loving support, we try to go it alone. We think we're strong, invincible, and in control! Not really.

Dig Deeper:

The title of Ecclesiastes in Hebrew means preacher or lecturer, implying that the author of the book has valuable lessons to teach us.

Where do we go for the support we need? To our friends or our spouse, of course, but first we should go to our Lord. Like the tall, strong cornstalk, he will guide us up and out of the misery and despair. Like the squash, he will provide a shield of protection against what might harm us. We can turn to him in prayer when we feel overwhelmed.

God wants us to have companionship. Isolation is not part of his plan. God, family, and friends. Like the cord of three strands and the three sister plants, together they will not be easily broken.

Background Bulb:

The Book of Ecclesiastes is one of the most pessimistic in the Old Testament, filled with despair over what life would be like without God. Most experts believe it was written by Solomon. King Solomon had a reputation for being wise, and as leader of Israel, his court was a center for all the best thinkers of his day. After a lifetime of seeking fulfillment in worldly things, Solomon repented. In Ecclesiastes he communicates from experience how pleasure, achievement, alcohol, riches, and sex all lead to emptiness without a good relationship with God.

Sprout & Scatter:

Trying to power through a project alone invites mistakes and burnout. We can benefit others and ourselves by asking for help. Identify one person who is lonely and invite her to join you in one of your duties or passions. You'll enjoy each other's company. The work will get done faster. And you will make a lasting impression on a person in need.

Think about it:

Why do you think that in the middle of all the despair written about in Ecclesiastes, the writer took time to write about the need for friends?

_____

_____

When was the last time you asked for help, and what was the result?

_____

_____

_____

Prayer Pot:

Lord, help me to ask for help when . . .

_____

_____

_____

_____

_____

_____

God is our friend who listens best.

You've Got Mail!

Today's Seed

> "Dear friends, this is now my second letter to you. I have written both of them as reminders to stimulate you to wholesome thinking."
>
> 2 Peter 3:1

Everyone loves to get mail. Letters from friends. Postcards from far-away places, saying, "Wish you were here." Invitations to weddings and parties. Announcements of engagements and graduations. Thank-you notes. Birthday cards. We love to get correspondence that says someone is thinking about us.

These days, handwritten correspondence is a lost art. While a dedicated few still take pen in hand and put their thoughts on paper, many of us rely on e-mail to get the message out. In an instant we can tell friends and family what's happening in our lives.

The apostle Peter wrote his letters to inform his recipients on a variety of doctrines and to remind them about Christian life and duties. In this second letter Peter warned about false teachers and encouraged watchfulness for the Lord's return. Peter emphasized that he felt the need to remind them to think good thoughts.

Dig Deeper:

The Greek word for "reminder" is *hupomnesis,* which means a remembrance. Sending a letter or e-mail to a friend reminds them that we remember them and think of them.

This was near the end of Peter's life, and he was compelled to write about the dangers he saw. False teachers, he said, worked from the inside to corrupt Christ's church. He encouraged Christians to remain committed to Christ and to live a holy life. Because Peter took time to write, we benefit from his letters.

Weed & Water:

Whether we take paper and pen in hand or use e-mail, it's the message not the method that counts. Share your thoughts, feelings, and compliments with friends and family; don't just pass along nonsense. When you know someone is hurting—either physically or emotionally—write a few kind words. Let them know they are in your thoughts and prayers. Tell them how much you appreciate them and how they have blessed you. Don't forget to write to your immediate family too.

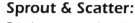

Sprout & Scatter:

Purchase or make attractive note cards—ones that say something about you and your likes and dislikes. Add a favorite, meaningful verse. Then address the envelope by hand, using a calligraphy pen. Put a pretty stamp on it, place a special sticker (flowers, animals, ladybugs, cats, dogs, or whatever appeals to you or the recipient) on the back envelope flap after it's sealed, and mail it. You'll make someone's day extra special. Write a letter to your child, telling them about the day they were born. Doing this blesses both the writer and the recipient.

Think about it:

Name some reasons Peter wrote his letters.

_____

_____

_____

How can you make your e-mails, letters, and cards more meaningful?

_____

_____

_____

_____

Prayer Pot:

Dear Lord, help me share my faith using the written word by . . .

_____

_____

_____

_____

_____

Send a letter today, sharing your faith.

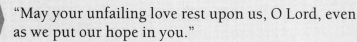

Hope

> "May your unfailing love rest upon us, O Lord, even as we put our hope in you."
>
> Psalm 33:22

Even though cedar-lined hope chests are not as popular as they once were, every girl dreams of the way things will be when she grows up. In her heart, hope has a home.

Christian hope is found in Jesus Christ. In him, we find evidence that God loves us. In him, there is confirmation of God's plan for our salvation and our lives. Because of him, we can face the sunrise tomorrow and the dark clouds that may come into our skies.

Because of Jesus we have reason to hope. When he makes a promise, our hearts believe it. Then our hope watches for it to happen. Doubting would be easier, but hope in Jesus overcomes doubt.

Your hope in Jesus will become most important to you when tragedy strikes. A great Scottish preacher said that the most profane word we use is hopeless because it slams the door in the face of God. When you face a crisis with your hope held high, your fears and panic will fade in its shadow. Clinging to hope is the ultimate act of faith.

Dig Deeper:

The Hebrew word for "hope" is *yachal,* which is also one of the Hebrew words for patience. Our hope is damaged when we fail to wait.

One of the reasons for our hope is that Jesus never gives up on us. Paul was confident in Jesus when he said, "He who began a good work in you will carry it on to completion until the day of Christ Jesus" (Philippians 1:6). What Jesus begins, he also finishes.

Background Bulb:

The other verses of Psalm 33 list some of the reasons that we have hope in God. They tell us that he is faithful in all he does. He created the world and is still in control. He looks down from heaven and considers everything we do. He has great strength. His plans stand firm forever. He is our help and our shield. We can trust in him because he is in control.

Sprout & Scatter:

Presenting Jesus to nonbelievers is difficult because they have already heard about religions, doctrines, and philosophies. Most people reject our attempts to convince them of our beliefs. But when you tell them about your hope, many will listen. Tell others what God has done for you in the past and why this gives you hope for the present and the future. Every heart yearns for hope.

Think about it:

List characteristics of God that give you hope?

🐞 _____

🐞 _____

🐞 _____

🐞 _____

How can you share your hope with a friend?

_____

_____

_____

_____

Prayer Pot:

Lord, help me trust you in . . .

_____

_____

_____

_____

_____

_____

Hang on to your hope especially in hopeless situations.

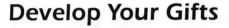

Develop Your Gifts

> "We have different gifts, according to the grace given us."
>
> Romans 12:6

As women, often we find ourselves facing a career choice at midlife. Whether it's because of a newly emptied nest or other life-changing circumstances, the question is the same: "What will I do?"

The will of God is identical for all believers in respect to holiness of life and completeness of dedication, but when it comes to our individual service in the church, it's a different story. Each of us has one or two spiritual gifts given to us by the grace of God. Unfortunately, we are often not aware of them, and so we haven't exercised them. We can get discouraged and think that we're too old or it's too late to develop them.

If we know our spiritual gift, we can be tempted to think we are better than others. Paul recognized how easily the possession of a particular gift could lead to pride. He cautioned believers to be humble and to keep from thinking one gift was better than another. Just as our body needs every part to function effectively,

Dig Deeper:

The Greek word for "gift," *charisma*, is derived from the word for grace, *charis*. Grace is undeserved favor, acceptance, and kindness from God. Our spiritual gift is a result of God's grace. We don't deserve it, and we can't earn it.

so the church needs all types of gifts to be healthy. Paul's goal in writing the above seed was to encourage Christians to use their gifts to the utmost in humility.

When Paul was asked if there was some gauge for measuring a person's position with regard to her gifts, he answered, "Yes, your faith." It is our measure of faith that determines the value of our gifts.

Weed & Water:

To discover your gift, find the common gift in the following three areas: (1) Make a list of the gifts you desire; (2) ask those who know you well to help you identify your gifts; and (3) consider your past volunteer experiences and the comments from others about what you did. Were you successful at teaching three-year-olds in Sunday school? Or did you do a great job organizing the last fund-raiser? If you are still unsure, get involved in a new activity at church to try out new skills or to test the gift you think you have.

Sprout & Scatter:

When we exercise our gifts, God's grace is dispensed to others. Encouragers lift up others. The merciful care for others, and teachers enlighten others. Whatever your gift, God has designed it to benefit others. Listen to your heart, and let God guide you to the best ministry for your gift.

Think about it:

What gift or gifts do you desire or need to develop?

_____

_____

_____

If the church is a body and your gift is lacking, how might the body be disabled?

_____

_____

_____

_____

Prayer Pot:

Lord, help me to focus on my gift and not be distracted by . . .

_____

_____

_____

_____

_____

_____

"God has created us with a tremendous drive to survive and a capability to succeed to the level of our God-given gifts."
— Marilyn Meberg

Change

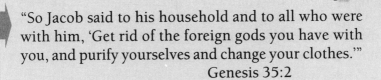

"So Jacob said to his household and to all who were with him, 'Get rid of the foreign gods you have with you, and purify yourselves and change your clothes.'"

Genesis 35:2

Change is never easy. From job transitions to moving far away from home, we resist and sometimes fear change. Jacob was moving his family to Bethel because God had given him instructions to go.

Jacob told his family that if they were going to change locations, they needed to change themselves too. He instructed them to throw away their foreign gods, clean up, and even change their clothes.

Like Jacob's family, we should throw away anything that might be keeping us from making the changes that God wants in our lives. If we rely on anything other than God, we are keeping "foreign gods." Luck, material possessions, and sometimes even our own abilities can become our gods.

Jacob asked his family to clean up their outward lives, but the real change he wanted for them is found in the next verse:

Dig Deeper:

The Hebrew word for "change" is *chalaph,* which is sometimes translated renew or sprout. The picture is of grass in the spring or a tree putting out new leaves. To really change is not merely getting rid of the old; it means being renewed or sprouting new growth.

"Then come, let us go up to Bethel, where I will build an altar to God . . ." (Genesis 35:3).

Jacob persuaded his family to stop the way they had been living and begin to worship God. Jacob had a great influence on his family and servants because he recognized that cleaning up the visible parts of our lives can only be meaningful if we also clean up the inside.

Background Bulb:

How could Jacob ask his family to make all these changes? Because he had been changed. He had been a deceiver and a thief when he tricked his brother to gain the family inheritance. He had run away from home. But God changed Jacob into a man of faith and courage because his heart was changed one night when he wrestled with God until dawn. God blessed him with new vision and courage for the future. He became the father of the nation of Israel.

Weed & Water:

We often work to change our appearance. Fitness magazines and videos and gyms are some of the fastest growing businesses in the United States. We want to look better and make a good impression. But a change in appearance will not change our bad attitudes or give us hope. Only a changed relationship with Jesus Christ can renew the person we are on the inside. Have you allowed him to throw away your old negative attitudes and change you into a positive courageous person?

Think about it:

Why might Jacob's family have been motivated to change when asked?

_____

_____

_____

Who has been the greatest influence in your life and helped you change?

_____

_____

_____

Prayer Pot:

Lord, help me not to fear change but to embrace opportunities . . .

_____

_____

_____

_____

_____

Changed people change people.

Respect the Elderly

Today's Seed

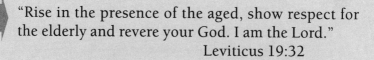

"Rise in the presence of the aged, show respect for the elderly and revere your God. I am the Lord."

Leviticus 19:32

There was a time when respect for the elderly was a given. Neighbors called older neighbors Mr. and Mrs. Smith instead of using their first names. Teenagers settled down when older people told them they were too rowdy in public. Children and adults listened to advice from older aunts and uncles. In business situations, counsel from the "old-timers" was heeded, and they were considered to be wise. Elders were, in a word, respected.

Although our society no longer respects the aged, God still wants Christians to value them. The Bible gives many examples of older people who played vital roles in Israel's history. Moses is one example.

When Moses was eighty, God sent him to rescue the Israelites from slavery in Egypt. After the people left Egypt, God gave Moses the long list of laws mentioned in Leviticus. These laws, such as, do not steal, do not lie, and do not hate, told the Israelites how God wanted them to live and worship. God showed the

Dig Deeper:

"Rise" in Hebrew not only means to get up from a sitting or lying position, but also to strengthen or to establish.

importance he placed on the elderly and how we should treat them by placing today's seed in the middle of this long list of laws. We need to remember that obeying God and treating others with respect is a way of showing respect for God.

Background Bulb:

Leviticus is a book of laws and regulations for worship. God gave the laws to Moses during the year that Israel camped at Mount Sinai. The phrase "I am the Lord" is used thirteen times in chapter 19. God wants us to know that he really means for us to obey these commands. He's not fooling around.

In Leviticus 19:10–31 most of the verses begin with the words "Do not." Verse 32 is a positive teaching rather than a prohibition. When we focus on what we can do rather than on what we shouldn't do, we'll discover that God's laws are for our good and for the good of those around us. It's a win-win situation.

Sprout & Scatter:

Here are some ideas to help you strengthen or establish the older people around you. Take the time to visit them. Listen to them. Interact with them. Ask their opinions. The elderly have much to teach us if we listen. If you have no elderly people in your life, borrow some. Adopt a grandmother or grandfather at an area nursing home or retirement village. Be cautious, though. You may not be able to keep up with him or her. Seniors today are running marathons, winning tennis tournaments, volunteering, and even working long past retirement age.

Think about it:

Why do you think God added "and revere your God" after telling us to show respect for the elderly?

_____

_____

_____

When was the last time you really listened to what an elderly person had to say?

_____

_____

_____

Prayer Pot:

Lord, help me to strengthen those who are older than me by . . .

_____

_____

_____

_____

_____

_____

Respect the elderly and receive a blessing.

Kindness

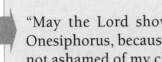

"May the Lord show mercy to the household of Onesiphorus, because he often refreshed me and was not ashamed of my chains."

2 Timothy 1:16

When driving through a tollbooth, several people discovered that some kind person ahead of them had paid their fee. Another person answered the doorbell only to find that a kind person had left a box of cookies on the doorstep. What a great feeling when someone is kind!

Onesiphorus exhibited kindness to Paul and was like a breath of fresh air when he came to visit him in prison. Kindness is refreshing in times of trouble. Paul was equally impressed that Onesiphorus was not ashamed that Paul was in jail. He came to see him anyway. His attention and kindness encouraged Paul.

Kindness can be as simple as a smile. In fact, most smiles are started by another smile. Missionaries tell how they can win the confidence of people with smiles even when they can't speak the language. They have learned the importance of a simple act of kindness like a smile. Kindness is also caring about others before

Dig Deeper:

The Greek word for "refreshed" is *anapsucho,* which means to cool off. In the heat of trouble, kindness is like a cool breeze.

we consider ourselves, making an effort when it's not convenient, and looking for a chance to do good.

This seed is part of a letter from Paul to Timothy, who was a young minister. He reminded Timothy of the qualities that Timothy needed to become a great preacher and pastor. When he mentioned the kindness of Onesiphorus, Paul showed Timothy kindness by example. When we see others being kind, it is an encouragement for us to develop kindness in our lives.

Background Bulb:

Paul was in jail because he had preached the gospel. The authorities didn't want him to continue. It must have seemed to Paul that everyone was against him. But Onesiphorus wouldn't give up on Paul. In verse 17 we are told that Onesiphorus searched everywhere to find Paul and came often to the jail. It wasn't the first time that Onesiphorus was kind to Paul. He had also helped him in Ephesus. The greatest kindness is repeated day after day even in the worst situations.

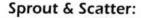

Sprout & Scatter:

Kindness is not kind unless it is expressed. If we are going to be kind, we must start by looking for chances to be kind. The opportunities are not hard to find. Help someone in the grocery store to reach an item. Call an elderly friend. Take a meal to a working mom. Buy a candy bar for a friend (unless she is on a diet). Mend or fix something. From taking the grocery cart back to the store to baking a special treat for your family, look for chances to be kind.

Think about it:

How has someone been kind to you?

_____

_____

_____

_____

What kind thing can you do today?

_____

_____

_____

_____

Prayer Pot:

Lord, give me an opportunity today to be kind to . . .

_____

_____

_____

_____

_____

_____

Kindness makes you feel good
whether it is done for you or by you.

Accountability

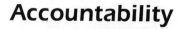

Today's Seed

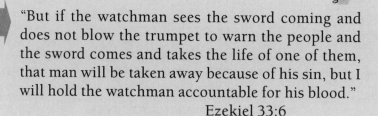

> "But if the watchman sees the sword coming and does not blow the trumpet to warn the people and the sword comes and takes the life of one of them, that man will be taken away because of his sin, but I will hold the watchman accountable for his blood."
>
> Ezekiel 33:6

Just reading this seed can cause us to shudder. We can be held accountable for not warning others of impending danger. That's quite a responsibility. Sin is the Christian's biggest danger. We might consider how our sins affect us, but how often do we consider how others' sins pose a danger to them? What's worse, we don't like the idea of having to warn them about it. But that's the basis of accountability.

Most of us have a hard enough time keeping ourselves accountable to God. Yet it is plain that God intended for us to support and to hold accountable those who are in our lives. It's easy for parents to expect children to be accountable, but it's harder to accept our duty of accountability to others. Another challenge is to allow

Dig Deeper:
The Complete Word Study Old Testament says the Hebrew word for "warn" means "to enlighten, teach; to warn, admonish, dissuade." Accountability encourages us to do good and keeps us from doing wrong so we may shine with God's glory. It also brings out the best in our friend.

others to hold us accountable, to accept constructive criticism. Accountability has two sides—giving advice and receiving it.

Friendship is one of the primary relationships where we should support one another by holding each other accountable. Instead, we often gossip or complain about the actions of a friend. That makes two who are doing the wrong thing. It takes courage to lovingly confront a friend and time to listen to her side, but if we make the effort we may succeed in warning a friend of danger.

Weed & Water:

God designed us as relational beings. Our relationships with him, our family, our church, and our friends should provide both defense and support. Therefore, we need to be careful in choosing our church and our friends. Proverbs 12:26 says, "A righteous man is cautious in friendship, but the way of the wicked leads them astray." It's easy to find "friends" that will commiserate with you and help justify wrong actions. It's a lot harder to choose friends that will honestly chastise you when you go astray.

Sprout & Scatter:

The best friendships are those where we can express our deepest fears and our most guarded secrets and where we can help someone else do the same. Ask a godly friend to be your accountability partner. Perhaps you can combine a weekly hour of walking with prayer, heart-to-heart talk, and wise counsel for mutual accountability.

Think about it:

List things that can happen if we fail to warn a friend of danger.

- _____
- _____
- _____

Which is harder for you—to give advice or to take it?

_____

_____

_____

_____

Prayer Pot:

Father, when I think about accountability, it is hard for me to . . .

_____

_____

_____

_____

_____

_____

The whole world will be held accountable to God.

Freedom from Worry

Today's Seed

> "Do not be anxious about anything, but in every-thing, by prayer and petition, with thanksgiving, present your requests to God."
>
> Philippians 4:6

Worrying can be all-consuming. It can eat us alive from the inside out. Worry feeds on itself. It starts small with the everyday things and grows into a monster, paralyzing our plans and our prayers.

Paul was in prison when he wrote to the Philippians. He had plenty of reasons to worry. He was probably physically chained to guards and was facing possible death. Yet in this letter to the Philippians, Paul uses the words "joy" and "rejoice" fourteen times.

Although Paul couldn't break out of prison, he had a mental attitude that was free as a bird. What was his secret?

The antidote to worry is "prayer and petition, with thanksgiving." Prayer is a worshipful talking with God, and petition means expressing our needs. Whenever we pray, we should be thankful; but thankfulness can be especially important when we are bogged down with worry. A spirit of thankfulness and a remembrance of past blessings pave the way for internal peace.

Dig Deeper:

The Greek word for "anxious" means fretful, overly concerned, to be pulled in different directions.

To be free of worry also implies a confidence in God's care and protection. Paul believed, as should we, that every circumstance in his life had occurred with God's knowledge and was under God's control. When we have a personal relationship with Christ, every experience of turning to him with our problems builds spiritual muscle with which to trust him in the future. His past provision is the foundation for our trust. From trust springs peace, and from peace comes joy.

Weed & Water:

The next time you are worrying . . .

Did I turn off the curling iron?

What are they going to find in the MRI results?

. . . Remember Paul's words to the people of Philippi. Tell God how you feel. Ask for his guidance about the issue. Then find one thing to be thankful for and build on that with more thanksgiving. Watch what happens. "The peace of God, which transcends all understanding, will guard your hearts and minds in Christ Jesus" (Philippians 4:7).

Sprout & Scatter:

Paul got his mind off himself by thinking about the people in Philippi. He did more than just think; he prayed for them and wrote them a letter. Paul demonstrates that one way to relieve worry is by earnestly asking God to act for the good of someone else. Think about someone who has a need, and then pray for him or her.

Think about it:

How does knowing Paul was in prison but not worried make you feel about your circumstances?

_____

_____

_____

List five things you can thank God for now.

🐞 _____

🐞 _____

🐞 _____

🐞 _____

🐞 _____

Prayer Pot:

Dear God, please take care of . . .

_____

_____

_____

_____

_____

_____

The antidote to worry is prayer and thanksgiving.

Love in Action

Today's Seed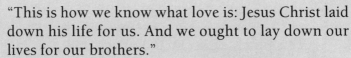

"This is how we know what love is: Jesus Christ laid down his life for us. And we ought to lay down our lives for our brothers."

1 John 3:16

A pop song from some time ago by the band Foreigner begins, "I want to know what love is." Most love songs talk about how the singer feels, with love being the ultimate emotion. In today's seed, John tells us what love is, and the picture he paints is very different from what's on TV or radio.

In today's culture, love means romance. We focus on finding that one true love, and we hope flowers, cards, and candy will be showered on us. We imagine that man will whisper "I love you" in our ear every day. We believe such love will give meaning to our lives.

Love does give meaning to our lives, but not the kind of love that is depicted in romance novels. The Bible puts little store in the words "I love you." Actions are what counts. They show our true heart. Love is not about feelings—it's about action.

Dig Deeper:

The Greek word for "love," *agape,* means benevolent love that is shown not by giving what the loved one *wants* but by doing what is *best* for the one loved. Only God can truly have this type of love, and we need his strength to enable us to love agape-style.

Look again at the way John phrased today's seed: Jesus laid down his life for us. In other words, Jesus' life was not taken from him by others. He chose to allow himself to be crucified. On purpose. For our sake.

How do we know what love is? Jesus died for us. It's that simple—and that profound. No matter how we feel, no matter what pain we endure, one thing we know: Jesus loves us—in both word and action.

Background Bulb:

The writer of 1 John is thought to be the apostle John, who also wrote the Gospel of John and Revelation. This "disciple whom Jesus loved" was the only apostle to live to a ripe old age; the others were martyred. Throughout his life John never stopped talking about love. According to one story, John often repeated, "Little children, love one another." People got tired of it and asked him why he said those words over and over. John replied, "Because it is the Lord's commandment, and if this be done it is enough."

Sprout & Scatter:

In the second part of the seed, John urges us to love others like Jesus loves us. Laying down our lives does not necessarily mean sacrificial death like it did for Jesus. We lay down our lives every time we sacrifice time, money, or our own wishes for the well-being of someone else. Today tell someone you love him or her and show your love by doing something nice for him or her.

Think about it:

How does reflecting on Jesus' life and death change your concept of love?

_____

_____

_____

What do your actions say about whom or what you love?

_____

_____

_____

Prayer Pot:

Lord, thank you for showing your love to me by . . .

_____

_____

_____

_____

_____

_____

"God demonstrates his love for us in this: While we were still sinners, Christ died for us."
—Romans 5:8

A Healthy Fear of God

*Today's
Seed*

> "He will be the sure foundation for your times, a rich store of salvation and wisdom and knowledge; the fear of the Lord is the key to this treasure."
> Isaiah 33:6

We'd all like to have a treasure trove of stability and a stash of salvation, wisdom, and knowledge. But at that word "fear" we stop, confused. What does it mean to fear the Lord?

Fear has two parts—to be afraid and to feel awe or reverence. A child who has eaten a forbidden cookie will be afraid when his mother comes into his room. His heart will race. He fears his sin will be discovered and punished. But moments later that same mother can use a batch of tools to fix his bike, and he will feel excited, surprised, and impressed that she can do such "magic."

To fear the Lord is to revere his name and to stand in awe of the one who created the universe and who has the power to sentence us to eternal death or life. The Bible often connects the fear of the Lord with obedience. A fear of punishment and respect for God's power can help us do what is right. Keeping God's commands brings benefits to us, as well as freedom from

Dig Deeper:

The word "reverence" appears in the Bible from Genesis to Revelation. Reverence comes from the Hebrew word *yare*. Reverence, combined with obedience, is a winning combination for believers.

the fear of punishment. A healthy fear means to love God and hold the Almighty in high esteem.

Israel had been disobedient and rebellious toward God. When they realized God's power and authority, they saw that he could deliver them. They bowed in reverence to the Lord. Through obedience they were allowed to receive deliverance. Justice and righteousness were promised as treasures! The key element was their fear of the Lord!

Background Bulb:

When Isaiah brought this message to Israel, the Assyrian army led by Sennacherib was attacking the city walls of Jerusalem, or Zion. Israel had hoped Egypt would come to their rescue, but those hopes had been dashed. Isaiah's words would have given comfort. God was all the people needed. He would protect them and give them wisdom for living. Although Sennacherib overtook other fortified cities in Judah, he could not take Jerusalem. His army was destroyed, and he was later assassinated by his sons.

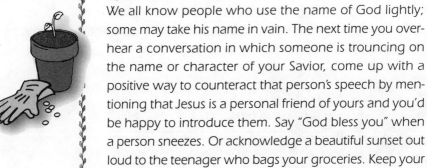

Sprout & Scatter:

We all know people who use the name of God lightly; some may take his name in vain. The next time you overhear a conversation in which someone is trouncing on the name or character of your Savior, come up with a positive way to counteract that person's speech by mentioning that Jesus is a personal friend of yours and you'd be happy to introduce them. Say "God bless you" when a person sneezes. Or acknowledge a beautiful sunset out loud to the teenager who bags your groceries. Keep your focus positive, and be nonthreatening.

Think about it:

On a scale of one to ten (one being the lowest), how would you rate your fear of the Lord?

_____

_____

_____

How can you bow in reverence to God?

_____

_____

_____

_____

Prayer Pot

Lord, I praise you for being my sure foundation. I praise you because . . .

_____

_____

_____

_____

_____

Healthy fear of God produces present benefits and future treasure.

God's Might

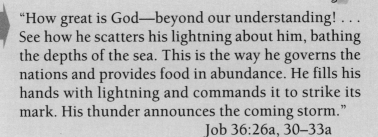

"How great is God—beyond our understanding! . . . See how he scatters his lightning about him, bathing the depths of the sea. This is the way he governs the nations and provides food in abundance. He fills his hands with lightning and commands it to strike its mark. His thunder announces the coming storm."

Job 36:26a, 30–33a

These verses are the first stanza of a hymn of praise for God's power. God's power and might is so amazing it is beyond our ability to understand. But anyone who has ever been outside during a storm has felt the power of thunder. Can you imagine being able to harness it in your bare hand? God fills his hands with lightning! He scatters it wherever he wants it to go.

God made the earth by his power, and he controls all the forces of nature. He alone has the power and ability to accomplish whatever he wills. He rules forever with his might. Yet he graciously stoops to use his power to help his children. By sending rain, God

Dig Deeper:

The Hebrew word for "command," *tsawah,* means make firm, establish, or decree. Although the word is used here for God commanding nature, it can also be used for a father giving instruction to a son, a farmer delegating orders to workers, and a king speaking decrees to subjects. With the ease that humans issue orders to subordinates, God controls nature.

nourishes the land and it produces crops to feed us. God uses his power in three different ways: to show his love, to punish, and for his own pleasure.

The same power that gives rain, ushers in the winter, and flashes the lightning is available to us. The Old Testament speaks of the "power of the Lord" coming upon individuals. Through the Holy Spirit, our God of Might grants supernatural strength to us when we are in need.

Think about how your heart pounds at the sight and sound of thunder and lightning. Compare this to the voice of God. His voice has dominion and power over all the earth. Imagine how our hearts will pound in heaven when we first hear his thundering voice!

Weed & Water:

As believers we can expect great things because of God's power at work within us. The same mighty strength that raised Jesus from the dead gives life to our bodies and spirits. The next time you are struggling with difficulties, think about what comes after the storm: clearing skies and brilliant sun. This too is symbolic of our God's golden splendor and awesome majesty.

Sprout & Scatter:

When the next electrical storm threatens, gather your family and read Job 36:26–33 to them. Talk about the images of God holding the lightning, scattering it, and bathing the sea with it. Watch the storm together from a safe spot. Ask your children to draw or paint an illustration of these verses. If your family has musical interests, make up a song using these verses.

Think about it:

Name some ways God shows his power.

- _____
- _____
- _____

How does knowing God controls nature make you feel about his control of your problems?

_____

_____

_____

_____

Prayer Pot:

Dear God, how great you are. I am impressed by your . . .

_____

_____

_____

_____

_____

_____

The God who holds lightning in his hands is the God who fills his heart with love for you.

It's Simple

Today's Seed

"Now all has been heard; here is the conclusion of the matter: Fear God and keep his commandments, for this is the whole [duty] of man."

Ecclesiastes 12:13

Have you noticed that not much is simple anymore?

Thanks to the computer and the computer chip, everything must be programmed in order to get it to work. You have to program the microwave (being careful not to change the time display) to just the right number of minutes so most of the kernels in the can't-see-through bag, pop. You can't watch television without knowing how to program your VCR. And if you have cable or satellite, you have five hundred or more channels to search through. Then there are the computer chips in the newer cars that do everything from locking the doors to giving you mile-by-mile directions to your destination. You can't even talk on the phone without listening to a series of options and punching several numbers on the Touch-Tone keypad.

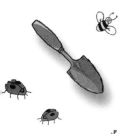

Dig Deeper:

The word used for "commandments" can be translated to describe God's laws, ordinances, and precepts. In other words, when speaking of God's commandments, more than the famous ten are included. Everything that pertains to us in God's Word from Genesis to Revelation is meant to be obeyed.

One thing in life is not complicated. Ironically, it's the thing about which many people experience stress. The uncomplicated thing is this: What does God expect from me? Solomon figured it out years ago. He wrote, "Fear God and keep his commandments, for this is the whole [duty] of man." It's simple.

Background Bulb:

King Solomon (who wrote the Book of Ecclesiastes) was the son of King David and Bathsheba. Having grown up with David as his father, he had seen firsthand the rights and responsibilities that follow the decisions kings make. From watching his father write psalms and songs, he may have learned that no matter how complicated things get around you, you can always withdraw to God.

Sprout & Scatter:

When your friends are harried because of the complications of life, encourage them to take a look at what really matters. The simple news is that God loves them. He longs for their love and wants them to have a heart that desires to obey his commandments.

Think about it:

What is complicated in your life right now?

_____

_____

_____

How can the message of this seed (love God and keep his commandments) speak to your complicated situation?

_____

_____

_____

Prayer Pot:

Lord, help me feel your love and apply your Word to my complicated life, especially when . . .

_____

_____

_____

_____

_____

"Our life is frittered away by detail . . . Simplify, simplify."
　　—Henry David Thoreau in
　　　　Where I Lived, and What I Lived For

Get a Guide

> "Whether you turn to the right or to the left, your ears will hear a voice behind you, saying, 'This is the way; walk in it.'"
>
> Isaiah 30:21

When you are in an unfamiliar city, the best investment you can make is a good map. It will keep you out of areas of danger and lead you to the interesting and fun places you want to see. We need a guide for our Christian life too, or we won't know what to do in times of trouble or when doubts arise.

Isaiah says that when we come to a crossroad of decision, we will hear instructions from behind us. Picture someone calling from behind as you walk down a path telling you what to expect around the next bend. This is what Isaiah means. But where do we get this kind of guide?

The first and most important guide is the Bible. The words in the Bible come directly from God to us and every word is true. As you study the Bible, you will find the path is clearly identified.

Dig Deeper:

The word "way" is translated from the Hebrew word *derek*. It means road or course of life. What a blessing to know that we can get on the right path with the counsel of God directing us!

Another guide is your conscience, but conscience is only a good guide when it has been soaked in the truths of the Bible. When God has taught our conscience, we can rely on it.

We can also count on godly people to act as a guide for us. Other Christians who have relied on God through troubled times can tell us what to do when we don't know which way to turn.

Weed & Water:

We might miss our way or be mistaken about which is the right way unless we get a guide. Notice how sure Isaiah is about the instructions we'll get from godly voices. "This is the way; walk in it" is emphatic and clear. In a world of uncertainty, God promises that we can be confident of our way when we get our instructions from him.

Sprout & Scatter:

These words of hope follow two promises that God made. First, there will be no more weeping. When we are sure of God's path, we don't need to be fearful or worried. Second, teachers will be present in our lives. Look around you. Are there people who have proven their faithfulness to God? If so, become a student of their words and actions. If not, ask God to bring someone into your life who will help you travel the right path.

Think about it:

What dilemma in your life makes you long for God's direction?

_____

_____

_____

What godly person can you rely on?

_____

_____

_____

_____

Prayer Pot:

Lord, *show me your path and I will follow . . .*

_____

_____

_____

_____

_____

_____

We seldom improve when we have no model but ourselves.

Be a Prepared Bride

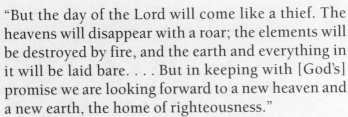

"But the day of the Lord will come like a thief. The heavens will disappear with a roar; the elements will be destroyed by fire, and the earth and everything in it will be laid bare. . . . But in keeping with [God's] promise we are looking forward to a new heaven and a new earth, the home of righteousness."

2 Peter 3:10, 13

Brides are never caught off guard by their wedding day. On the other hand, robbery victims are always shocked by a theft. Brides are joyfully prepared. Robbery victims are horrified. Depending on our level of preparation, the Second Coming of the Lord will cause one of these two reactions: joy or shock.

In the third chapter of Peter, the author talks about the final judgment of the wicked, the end of the world as we know it, and the new heaven and earth. All believers will receive their reward of heaven and joyful life with God. Of this we can be certain.

Dig Deeper:

This seed says, "the heavens will disappear with a roar." The Greek word for "roar" is only used once in the New Testament. It is a colorful word from the root *rhoizos*, which means the noise made by something whizzing through the air. Easily and in a flash, God will destroy this world.

But just as certain is the end of this world. It is doomed. The sky will disappear, the things that make up the earth's matter will be destroyed, and all the works of people will be burned up.

Believers can rest in the knowledge of a wonderful afterlife with God. The new heaven and earth will have no disease, suffering, pain, sorrow, or death. All the ravages of sin and the effects of the fall will be gone. Evil will be destroyed. It will be so wonderful and beautiful we cannot adequately describe it using words of this world. Isaiah 11:6 says, "The leopard will lie down with the goat, the calf and the lion and the yearling together; and a little child will lead them."

In that great day believers—the prepared—will become the bride of Christ.

Weed & Water:

Just as a bride is thoroughly prepared for her wedding, so we are to be prepared for Christ's coming. Peter explains how believers should live. Here are some of his ideas: Be godly by worshiping God in truth. Act holy by being separate from evil. Look forward to Christ's coming. Be diligent to be found spiritually spotless and blameless. Be on guard against false teachers. Grow in grace and knowledge of God.

Sprout & Scatter:

Don't be impatient when Christ's Second Coming seems to be slow in arriving. Know that God is waiting so that more people can be saved. We can help to bring this about by praying for those who don't know Christ, by being good examples of what it means to be a Christian, and by telling others about the hope they can have in Jesus.

Think about it:

How can you prepare for Christ's Second Coming?

_____

_____

_____

What do you look forward to in the new heaven and earth?

_____

_____

_____

_____

Prayer Pot:

Lord, your power amazes me. Help me prepare for your coming by . . .

_____

_____

_____

_____

"[God] will wipe every tear from their eyes. There will be no more death or mourning or crying or pain, for the old order of things has passed away."
Revelation 21:4

About the Contributors

Rondi DeBoer, author of eight books for children and adults, holds a graduate certificate in Bible from Multnomah Biblical Seminary. She and her husband live in Spokane, Washington, and are the parents of one young daughter. (16, 55, 103, 142, 160)

Jennifer Gross has led small groups and served as evangelism director for her church. She writes newsletters on college admissions and is the author of *Wizdom: A Kit of Wit and Wisdom for Kids with Diabetes (and their Parents)*. Her lifelong struggle with procrastination has led her to focus on how to put God's Word into practice *today*. (250)

Pat Johnson is special features editor for the Lancaster (Pennsylvania) newspapers. Widowed at age forty-two, she raised three children and now enjoys four grandchildren. A freelance photographer, Pat has also written for many magazines, take-home papers, and devotionals. Currently, she is working on a romantic mystery. (7, 19, 31, 37, 46, 49, 52, 64, 79, 88, 94, 109, 121, 124, 130, 136, 145, 148, 157, 169, 175, 178, 184, 187, 190, 196, 199, 205, 211, 223, 226, 238, 247)

Sharon Norris is a published author and popular speaker who touches the lives of her audiences at conferences, women's retreats, seminars, church, and school programs. She teaches high school English and journalism in Inglewood, California. Sharon is a single mother of two middle school sons. (13, 58, 100, 166, 172, 202, 259)

Karen Porter is a freelance writer, Bible teacher, and inspirational speaker from Texas. She is vice president of international marketing of a major food company.

She has been published in a variety of magazines including *Discipleship Journal* and has written Sunday school curriculum for Lifeway. (1, 28, 34, 40, 61, 76, 82, 118, 139, 151, 163, 181, 193, 214, 217, 229, 235, 241, 262)

Sharon Hanby-Robie, a lifelong Christian, became even closer to God years ago when he healed her of cancer at the age of twenty-eight. She is vice president of marketing at Starburst Publishers, a speaker, television personality, and the author of *My Name Isn't Martha But I Can Decorate My Home* series of books. She and her husband live with their two cats and enjoy relating to nine nieces and nephews. (22, 70, 85, 112, 115, 154, 232, 244, 256)

Betty Southard is a Bible teacher, adjunct professor at Biola University, on the teaching staff for Christian Leaders, Authors and Speakers Seminars, and coauthor of two books: *The Grandmother Book* and *Come As You Are.* The married mother of three grown daughters and grandmother of seven, Betty has a master's degree in theology from Fuller Seminary. (4, 43, 67, 73, 91, 106, 127, 133)

Deb Strubel, editor at Starburst Publishers, has taught Sunday school and Precept Bible studies. The married mother of two teens, she has been published in national Christian magazines and is the coauthor of *Single, Whole and Holy: Christian Women and Sexuality.* (10, 265)

Denine Ziegler is passionate about ministering to today's youth culture. Her byline appears regularly in the *Kutztown (Pennsylvania) Patriot, Vocational Biographies,* and *Berks County Living Magazine.* Married for sixteen years, Denine is the mother of two teenagers. (25, 97, 208, 220, 253)

Scripture Index

Old Testament

Boldface references indicate those that appear at the beginning of a study-devotional. All other references appear within the lesson texts.

New Testament

Subject and Name Index

POPULAR BOOKS BY
STARBURST PUBLISHERS®

Bible Seeds: A Simple Study-Devotional for Growing in God's Word
From the Creators of the God's Word for the Biblically-Inept™ *Series*
Growing your faith is like tending a garden—just plant the seed of God's Word in your heart, tend it with prayer, and watch it blossom. At the heart of this unique study is a Bible verse or "seed" that is combined with an inspirational lesson, a word study, application tips, thought questions with room to write, a prayer starter, and a final thought.
(trade paper) ISBN 1892016443 **$13.99**

Bible Bytes for Teens: A Study-Devotional for Logging In to God's Word
From the Creators of the God's Word for the Biblically-Inept™ *Series*
Growing up isn't easy in today's fast-paced world of e-this and i-that. Now, teens can exit off the information superhighway with a bit of the Bible. Each two-page lesson starts with an anecdote about an issue relevant to teens, includes a Bible verse, easy-to-understand devotional lesson, questions for application, and a power-packed takeaway.
(trade paper) ISBN 1892016494 **$13.99** (Available May 2001)

The *God's Word for the Biblically-Inept™* series is already a best-seller with over 150,000 books sold! Designed to make reading the Bible easy, educational, and fun! This series of verse-by-verse Bible studies, topical studies, and overviews mixes scholarly information from experts with helpful icons, illustrations, sidebars, and time lines. It's the Bible made easy!

Women of the Bible—God's Word for the Biblically-Inept™
By Kathy Collard Miller
Finally, a Bible perspective just for women! Gain valuable insight from the successes and struggles of such women as Eve, Esther, Mary, Sarah, and Rebekah. Interesting icons like "Get Close to God," "Build Your Spirit," and "Grow Your Marriage" will make it easy to incorporate God's Word into your daily life.
(trade paper) ISBN 0914984063 **$16.95**

The Bible—God's Word for the Biblically-Inept™
By Larry Richards
An excellent book to start learning the entire Bible. Get the basics or the in-depth information you are seeking with this user-friendly overview.
(trade paper) ISBN 0914984551 **$16.95**

John—God's Word for the Biblically-Inept™
By Lin Johnson
From village fisherman to beloved apostle, John was an eyewitness to the teachings and miracles of Christ. Now, readers can join in an easy-to-understand, verse-by-verse journey through the fourth and most unique of all the gospels.
(trade paper)   ISBN 1892016435   **$16.95**

• **Learn more at www.biblicallyinept.com** •

The **What's in the Bible for . . .**™ series focuses its attention on making the Bible applicable to everyday life. Whether you're a teenager or senior citizen, this series has the book for you! Each title is equipped with the same reader-friendly icons, call-outs, tables, illustrations, questions, and chapter summaries that are used in the *God's Word for the Biblically-Inept™* series. It's another easy way to access God's Word!

What's in the Bible for . . .™ **Women**
By Georgia Curtis Ling
Women of all ages will find biblical insight on topics that are meaningful to them in four sections: Wisdom for the Journey; Family Ties; Bread, Breadwinners, and Bread Makers; and Fellowship and Community Involvement.
(trade paper)   ISBN 1892016109   **$16.95**

What's in the Bible for . . .™ **Mothers**
By Judy Bodmer
Is home schooling a good idea? Is it okay to work? At what age should I start treating my children like responsible adults? What is the most important thing I can teach my children? If you are asking these questions and need help answering them, *What's in the Bible for . . .*™ *Mothers* is especially for you!
(trade paper)   ISBN 1892016265   **$16.95**

*What's in the Bible for . . . *™ **Couples**
By Larry and Kathy Miller
Restore love, unity, and commitment with internationally acclaimed relationship experts Larry and Kathy Miller as they explore God's Word on such topics as dating, sex, money, and trauma. Don't miss the "Take It from Them" feature, which offers wisdom from couples who have lived and learned, and the "Couples of the Bible" feature that spotlights the experiences of such couples as Adam and Eve, Abraham and Sarah, and Joseph and Mary.
(trade paper)   ISBN 1892016028   **$16.95**

An Expressive Heart: Stories, Lessons, and Exercises Inspired by Psalms
Edited by Kathy Collard Miller
An intimate book of inspirational lessons from the best-selling editor of the *God's Abundance* collection. Each selection includes a passage from the poetic Book of Psalms, an inspirational story with a lesson, quotation, and journaling idea. There's even room to write. The Psalms provide an unmatched guide for anyone who wants to know God better, and *An Expressive Heart* will help you give words to your feelings.
(trade paper) ISBN 1892016508 **$12.99**   (Available April 2001)

Purchasing Information
www.starburstpublishers.com

Books are available from your favorite bookstore, either from current stock or special order. To assist bookstores in locating your selection, be sure to give title, author, and ISBN. If unable to purchase from a bookstore, you may order direct from STARBURST PUBLISHERS. When ordering please enclose full payment plus shipping and handling as follows:

Post Office (4th class)
$4.00 with purchase of up to $20.00
$5.00 ($20.01–$50.00)
8% of purchase price for purchases of $50.01 and up

Canada
$5.00 (up to $35.00)
15% ($35.01 and up)

United Parcel Service (UPS)
$5.00 (up to $20.00)
$7.00 ($20.01–$50.00)
12 % ($50.01 and up)

Overseas
$5.00 (up to $25.00)
20% ($25.01 and up)

Payment in U.S. funds only. Please allow two to four weeks minimum for delivery by USPS (longer for overseas and Canada). Allow two to seven working days for delivery by UPS. Make checks payable to and mail to:

Starburst Publishers®
P.O. Box 4123
Lancaster, PA 17604

Credit card orders may be placed by calling 1-800-441-1456, Mon.–Fri., 8:30 A.M. to 5:30 P.M. Eastern Standard Time. Prices are subject to change without notice. Catalogs are available for a 9 x 12 self-addressed envelope with four first-class stamps.

Understanding the Bible is Just a Click Away!

Starburst Publishers brings you the best internet sites for homeschool, Sunday School, and individual or group Bible study!

www.biblicallyinept.com

View our FREE weekly Bible study on-line or have it delivered to your email address at no charge! It's the *What the Bible Says about . . .*™ weekly Bible study from Dr. Larry Richards, General Editor of the best-selling *God's Word for the Biblically-Inept*™ series.

www.homeschoolteach.com
www.sundayschoolteach.com

Each of these two sites offers a FREE e-newsletter with resources, fresh ideas, activities, news updates, and more! You will also find the internet's first downloadable homeschool and Sunday School Bible curriculums!

The Bible Made Easy!